Title: "The Baby Business Success  economic trends shaping the U.S. and the best businesses to start today!

Unleash your Hidden Potential: Great Ideas for Careers and Small-Businesses

25 Future Trends that will shape the small business landscape!

I) Preface: The American Dream

It's time for every working American to take a close look at their career and their prospects for staying employed in today's unforgiving job market.

The events taking place in corporate America are changing daily. Everywhere you look today companies are downsizing, rightsizing, outsourcing or off-shoring workers.

The cold, hard reality is that many companies are looking to replace workers through automation and technology.

Take a look at the common themes in today's headlines.

"Economists worry economy won't recoup 7 million lost jobs". "Experts don't really see an end in sight for the economy to regain those lost jobs and the unemployment rate will remain stubbornly high".

If you are part of the baby boomer you are part of the greatest generation! 76 million strong and redefining the way you work and live for generations to follow. The word "retirement" seems like an oxymoron today. The economy seems to have lost its way. Jobs are being lost, people are losing their homes everyday and it seems the American dream is slipping away for many Americans.

If you've picked up this book, don't put it down as it could be the beginning of the next great chapter in your life.

The American Dream of starting and running your own business is one held by many Americans today. A recent survey recently suggested that 72% of Americans would like to start their own business. Are you one of the 72%? We live in the greatest nation on earth, with endless possibilities and opportunities. There really has been no better time in history to start your own business. Thousands of immigrants from all over the world land on our shores each day to seek out their piece of the American Dream. They know instinctively that America is the only place on earth where they can fulfill this desire.

With the right level of passion, drive and ambition you can make the dream a reality.

This dream holds no boundaries. Major universities across the U.S. now recognize entrepreneurship as a viable course of study and offer it as a recognized degree. Retired baby boomers look at entrepreneurship as a way toward pursuing a passion they've had their entire life. An article in the *Atlanta Journal Constitution* had this to say about the upcoming wave of new start up businesses by the baby boomer generation. "By all appearances, the wave of boomer entrepreneurship has already started". "This time around, however, the burst in entrepreneurial activity will not be led by twenty-something's," the report suggested, "but by baby boomers and would-be retirees in their 40s, 50s, 60s and even 70s, who are better educated, healthier and more tech-savvy than their predecessors."

The reason this phenomenon is occurring is multi-faceted. First and foremost, many baby boomers want to stay active in their retirement years. Many of them have worked for corporations and they have gained valuable skills and experiences that could translate to a small company. Some boomers had the "dream" of starting a business for many years, but got saddled with mortgage payments, college tuition and other expenses and now that they've reached a point were most of those expenses are diminished or gone, they have the opportunity to pursue something for themselves.

Many of the articles I've written in *Startup Nation.com* and Second50years.com discuss the need to look at current and emerging trends in the marketplace. This is one of the most key, fundamental aspects of starting a business. You may have an idea or a concept about a particular business that may sound wonderful to you, but if you can't connect it to a future need or trend in a particular consumer segment the business won't have legs to stand on.

Most people don't take the time to do their homework and research regarding this important decision. I believe the most important first step you can do toward your goal of starting your business, is to connect a trend to something you really enjoying doing. If you can connect these two together, it will become a recipe for success.

When you look at certain markets or industries such as technology, healthcare, entertainment and the changing U.S. demographics, they will reveal great opportunities for small business start-ups. If you don't catch these trends early, you could be missing out on a great chance to create a successful, thriving business well into the future! We can trace trends to opportunity over and over again throughout history. Take for example the trend started in fast food restaurants in the mid-1950's. You know what franchise I'm talking about. McDonald's restaurant, the leader in fast food empires kicked off the franchising trend, which has spawned thousands of franchises across the globe. Consumers simply wanted quick food that was inexpensive and easy to get no matter where they lived. McDonald's simply capitalized on this trend. Fast-forward to 2005. Who would have thought a company called Starbucks could charge $3.00 for a cup of coffee, when you can buy a whole pound at the grocery store for the same price. Starbuck's tied into a trend where people identified with an upscale brand of coffee that made a statement about their lives and who they were as an individual. When a company ties into that need among consumers, it truly creates a level of brand loyalty with its customer's.

If you are in the beginning stages of deciding what small business to start, don't leave it up to chance. Take the time and research which businesses have the most chance of succeeding before you take the leap.

"The Baby Boomers Guide to Small Business Success" is packed with useful information on which businesses make the most sense and which one's will provide the highest level of success based on current and future trends in the marketplace. It also discusses how to use your skills and talents to match those to a business that is right for you.

Let this book be your first stop on your road to success!

If you are currently in a career transition and are looking for your next opportunity, don't overlook the possibility of self-employment. Many people think when they are down-sized; their first thought is "how do I get another job"? They put all their time and energy into finding the very thing that may have contributed to losing their job in the first place. Take a look at your talents and experience. Where might those skills translate to self-employment? How can you match current trends with your skills? You may be pleasantly surprised to learn that you have the right skills and experience to start a venture on your own.

Most of us, when we were young were taught: "go to school, get good grades and get a job", the paradigm and work ethic of the baby boomer generation. We were told this would lead to a successful career and happy retirement. I think in today's market we are creating an illusion of what is real by fostering this belief system. The formula that worked during that generation does not work in today's 21st century marketplace.

It's important to recognize the changes that are taking place in today's marketplace and to look at how you can create sources of income in which you control. I firmly believe that each of us needs to recognize the need to be more independent and to develop ways to leverage our talents, abilities and creativity as we move into the 21st century. The timing has never been better as new and wondrous opportunities are beginning to emerge setting up an environment to create a thriving small business.

I've designed this book as a way to instill ideas and to provoke thinking as to how you can harness your specific talents, spot emerging trends and then execute a plan to accomplish your goals. It doesn't matter if you are twenty, forty or sixty! The same principle apply regardless if you are working, retired, or in transition or about to enter another phase of your career.

Table of Contents:

I) Preface: The American Dream

II) The Headlines: The Constant Changing Job Market

III) Establishing Value through Creativity and Observation

IV) Transforming Creativity into Business Reality

V) Trends in the Marketplace

VI) 21st Century Business Opportunities

VII) Controlled risk-taking coupled with innovation

VIII) Fostering innovation and creativity

IX) Don't quit your day job

X) A Closer Look at Franchising

XI) It's all about Marketing!!!!

XII Finding an outlet for your creativity

XIII) Conclusion

II) The Headlines: The Constant Changing Job Market

We all read the headlines each day about job losses, outsourcing, downsizing, employee dissatisfaction, and corporate scandal. Let's face it, these are trying times! Job security and loyalty from both employer and employee has suffered dramatically in the last 20 years.

Workers and current job seekers alike are perplexed at the ever-changing job market!

There is a simple truth today when working for others. And that is you really don't have any guarantee the job you have today will be there tomorrow. I won't bore you with all the overwhelming statistics on companies that are downsizing, outsourcing and consolidating job functions. The good news, though, is that it is motivating people to act. There really is no better time to look into self-employment. The opportunities I talk about discuss the top twenty-five trends occurring in the marketplace today. The technology available today allows a small businessperson to look like their bigger counterparts. Many companies today would rather use smaller firms to do a lot of the things they used to do in-house, which in turn creates more opportunity for smaller businesses. Small businesses today create most new jobs. Secretary of Labor, Elaine L. Chao is quoted, "Employment, Jobs Creation and Innovation. That's the value of small business to our country".. President Bush's agenda on small business says a lot about the connection between job creation and small business, "In fact, small and young companies create two thirds of the net new jobs in our economy, and they employ half of all private-sector workers. Entrepreneurship has become the path to prosperity for many Americans, including minorities and women".

Many of us today hear the term "outsourcing" and we want to stick our heads in the sand and pretend it doesn't exist. The fact is, outsourcing is here and it's not going away anytime soon. The question will be how will you deal with this new reality so you or your income is not affected? One way is to create real value and not the illusion of value. Customers will pay for lasting true value they can't get anywhere else. If you create a business with this goal in mind and don't lose sight of the customer in all that you do, you really won't have any worries about outsourcing.

What we are seeing is the globalization of the world's work force, which by many accounts is still in the early stages. The effect from this globalization has allowed employers to drastically lower labor costs, giving them more flexibility and freedom in hiring. The fallout is a more competitive and brutal job market including stagnant and declining pay. Presently, the number of jobs lost represents a fraction of the total labor market at 2.5%. However, many labor experts agree that off shoring will grow rapidly, becoming a permanent way for companies to do business. As the amount of jobs vulnerable to off shoring increases, many Americans will migrate to other fields like healthcare and education, which require face-to-face contact. Many jobs that are being outsourced are routine jobs or jobs that can be easily replicated in places like India. Routine jobs, such as programming and documentation writing are a few in the IT realm that qualify within this category.

The demise of old industries and the creation of new ones is a pattern often repeated in U.S. history. The American economy's ability to regenerate itself-from an agricultural to industrial and eventually a service-oriented economy has made us the envy of the world. Companies, determined to remain competitive, are outsourcing jobs to India and other countries where labor is cheaper. And the jobs they are shipping out are not limited to low-level, blue collar roles; they include white-collar positions traditionally thought to be untouchable outside the U.S. Automation is also playing a big role in allowing companies to do more with less. This rise in technology has virtually eliminated low-level jobs such as supermarket cashiers, airport ticket agents and bank tellers. Jobs that used to be the American backbone and one's that could be counted on for many Americans have gone the way of the dinosaur. Companies pleased with the results and cost-savings measures will continue to look for ways to cut out jobs that can be replaced through automation. No job will be sacred any longer! The move to outsource and eliminate jobs will take out huge parts of the U.S. wage structure. Forrester Research has forecast that nearly 10 million U.S. jobs will move off shore between years 2003 through 2015. These white-collar jobs will range from office and computer work to management, sales and architecture. A further study estimates that 14 million jobs are at risk. Some of these jobs, in such fields as software, technical writing and translation, and financial analysis could be at risk. As the educational and technological gaps between the United States, India and China and other developing countries begin to narrow, labor market experts say U.S. workers will fall into two categories. At one end will be a supply of low-paying jobs such as teaching and retail sales. These positions require direct personal interaction, not a voice on the other end of the phone line or an email. Wal-Mart alone will create more than 415,000 jobs in the United States over the next five years.

On the other side of the spectrum, there will be fewer high-paying jobs such as software project managers and information systems security professionals. These jobs involve complex tasks that can't be performed offshore because they often entail handling sensitive information. Many "new" jobs are expected to spring from the fields of healthcare and education. The Bureau of Labor Statistics estimates that one out of every four jobs created in the United States between 2002 and 2012 will be in health care and social assistance or private educational services. Among the most job openings: registered nurses and primary, secondary and special education teachers. The five-fastest growing occupations include medical assistants, physician assistants and home health aides.

One interesting note to keep in mind is the constant emphasis on a "job". The article mentions nothing about the creation of business opportunities through entrepreneurship. The article suggests very clearly that if you want a "job" in the next 6-8years, you will need to focus within the fields of healthcare and teaching. That is all well and good for those seeking employment, however, I strongly believe we have to cultivate more of a spirit of innovation, business creation and ownership in this country. We've got to start taking ownership and realizing "jobs" are not going to be here for many of us going forward. The skills you learned under the old paradigm during your college years no longer apply.

Entrepreneurship can become a way of life for many people.

If you are skeptical about this shift from worker to entrepreneur, and why the need exists, think about the successful television show, "The Apprentice", which debuted in 2004 and stars Donald Trump who imparts his business wisdom to a group of young and ambitious entrepreneurs who take responsibility for creating successful business opportunities under Trump's tutelage!

This television show illustrates America's fascination with the process of taking ordinary people and enabling them to create something from virtually nothing! They are using sheer innovation and creativity to reach their goals to create income for themselves. It embodies the American dream that symbolizes this country and taps into a very real desire that people have to break away from the bonds that hold them to an organizational corporate structure.

Former Chairman Alan Greenspan stated, "We need to start teaching financial literacy in our schools". We need to start teaching our children to take care of themselves financially, rather than teaching them to expect the government or a company to take care of them after they retire. Also worth nothing is that 7 million jobs have been lost within the U.S. economy since December 2007.

I have had many friends, colleagues, peers who have been devastated by loss of jobs, income, and security and to a small extent their credit, homes and personal assets have been impacted. I'm saying a paradigm shift is taking place were none of the old rules apply anymore and we need to educate our children early on how they can best prepare for a world that rewards creativity, entrepreneurship and controlled risk-taking.
We need to raise children's awareness with these "new set of core values". "The times, they are a changin' per Bob Dylan.

III) Establishing Value through Creativity

It's helpful to think about how many examples we can seek out in every day life that exemplifies how we can incorporate everyday observations into business reality. Let's take a look at several prominent individuals who established value through creativity and what they had to say about success and failure in their endeavors:

Can you match the quotes to these famous individuals?

1). "You may get skinned knees and elbows, but it's worth it if you score a spectacular goal."

2). "Press on. Nothing in the world can take the place of persistence."

3). "It is fine to celebrate success, but it is more important to learn the lessons of failure."

4). "I take rejection as someone blowing a bugle in my ear to wake me up and get going rather than retreat."

5). "I never failed once. It just happened to be a 2,000 step process."

6). "Success is not final. Failure is not fatal. It is the courage to continue that counts."

7). "Most of the important things in the world have been accomplished by people who have kept on trying when there seemed to be no hope at all."

8). "Sometimes when you innovate you make mistakes. It is best to admit them quickly and get on with improving your other innovation."

9). "Never let the fear of striking out get in your way."

10). "What separates the winners from the losers is how a person reacts to each new twist of fate."

See answers below:

1). Mia Hamm, U.S. Women's Olympic Soccer champ

2). Ray Kroc, Founder of McDonald's

3). Bill Gates, Founder of Microsoft

4). Sylvester Stallone, Actor

5). Thomas Edison, Inventor

6). Winston Churchill, Prime Minister, England

7). Dale Carnegie, Author, Motivational Speaker

8). Steve Jobs, CEO, Apple Computers

9). Babe Ruth, Baseball Player

10). Donald Trump, Real Estate Mogul

These famous individuals established value through creativity. They took advantage of their surroundings and their environment and found opportunity. It may seem intimidating to put yourself in the same category as the people mentioned above, however, there really is no need to feel this way. These people started out just like you. They weren't well known or famous when they started. They had a dream, an idea and had the courage to follow that dream and made sure it became a reality. All of us have it within ourselves to do the very same thing. Don't underestimate yourself because you aren't "famous" or "well-known." Remember, they weren't either when they first started out.

The following information was extracted from the "Learning Web" "For employment, in particular, small companies are vital. Says John Naisbitt: "It's the young entrepreneurial companies that are creating nearly all the new jobs in the United States. In the 1980s America created 22 million brand-new jobs; there were that many more people in paid employment at the end of the eighties. And 90 percent of those 22 million jobs were in companies of 50 or fewer employees. That is the new economy. That is what's creating the new wealth-creating capacity. So if you want to see what the new company looks like, you look at the young companies, not the old household-word companies that are shrinking and are very slow to change."

In many of these companies, the educational need is for thinking and conceptual skills, risk-taking, experimenting, and openness to change and opportunity.

Leisure, tourism and lifelong education will be among the major growth industries. Already some of the trends are obvious. Half a billion tourists travel each year. By the year 2000, the prediction is a billion.

Overcrowded Japan set goals in the mid-1980s to have 10 million of its citizens taking holidays abroad by 1991. The target was achieved. Over 90 percent of Japanese newlyweds honeymoon in other countries.

In Florida, 33 million visitors a year now flock into the former swampland of Orlando - thanks to the vision of Walt Disney and the planning of his successors. More than 55 million tourists from other countries visit France each year, and the 23.6 million who visited Britain in 1995 spent $17.5 billion. London's main airport at Heathrow is now also a major shopping center, with a retail turnover of $500 million a year.

Just as economies are dramatically changing, so are demographics. And the most striking trend in developed countries is the active aging of the population.

A hundred years ago only 2.4 million Americans were over 65, under four in every 100. Today there are over 30 million - around one in eight. By 2050: over 67 million - almost 22 percent of the population. Since 1920, in America, average life expectancy has increased from 54 years to 75. In most developed countries, with the notable exception of Russia, the average male reaching 60 can also expect to live to at least 75 and the average woman over 80.

At current rates of growth, by the year 2025, the world's over-60 population will have increased to one billion. Little wonder that many are calling 60-plus *The Third Age*. Others are challenging us to abolish the word "retirement" from our vocabularies.

Thomas Edison held 1,093 patents, and electrified the world. Walt Disney and Apple Computers' Steve Jobs each founded giant commercial empires on the power of a new idea - and a different make-believe mouse. Ray Kroc was a middle-aged milk-shake machine salesman when he first visited the California hamburger bar of Dick and Maurice McDonald. He was to take their basic concept, mix it with others, and turn the result into the world's biggest fast-food chain. Georgi Lozanov, the Bulgarian psychologist, linked yoga, meditation and music to revolutionize the teaching of foreign languages. The Internet and World Wide Web have completely changed the way the world communicates.

Bill Gates is the richest man in America firstly because he and his partner, Paul Allen, had a dream to put a computer on every desk and in every home.

The two richest men in Europe owe their wealth to their father, Richard Rausing. While watching his wife prepare homemade sausages, he became intrigued by how she peeled back the skins to insert the ingredients. That idea turned into the system of pouring milk from cartons, and his heirs still receive royalties every day from millions of Tetrapak milk cartons.

All the great ideas in history, all the great inventions, obviously have one thing in common. All have come from the human brain. Just as the brain has fantastic ability to store information, it has an equal ability to reassemble that information in new ways: to create new ideas.

And very simply, an idea is a new combination of old elements. Write that down, underline it, and reinforce it. It could be the most important sentence you ever write. It contains the key to creating new solutions. There are no new elements. There are only new combinations.

Think for a moment of the thousands of different cookbooks around the world. Every recipe in every book is a different mixture of existing ingredients. Think of that example whenever you tackle a problem. And all the breakthroughs everywhere - radio, television, the internal combustion engine - are new combinations of old bits. A push-button shower combines at least three "old" elements: hot and cold water and a mixing valve. Nylon and other "new" synthetic fibres are new combinations of molecules that have existed for hundreds of centuries. In nylon's case: they are recombined molecules from coal.

Since an idea is a new mixture of old elements, the best ideas-creators are constantly preoccupied with new combinations.

In most management courses, you learn the overriding need to define correctly the problem you want solved. But now a new revolutionary element has emerged. We can now define the ideal solution in advance - and start creating it.

This is a revolutionary change. Whereas previously we organized our existing knowledge to solve a problem, within the limits of that knowledge, today we start by defining what we would like to achieve. And then we organize the things we don't know in order to achieve it. Sixty years ago clothing manufacturers were stuck with such basic yarns as wool, cotton and silk. Then Wallace Corothers synthesized nylon in 1935. Today we can define the ideal garment, and then produce the fibers and mixtures to create it. Families became tired of darning socks, so science created a blend of nylon and wool to give us the benefit of both: a new mixture of old elements.

Iron-weary mothers wanted shirts that would drip-dry without creases. So science created polyester fibers: a new combination of old elements.

Fashion-conscious women liked the easy-care properties of nylon but pined for the fluffiness of wool. Science created acrylics - by recombining the elements of natural gas. Peter Drucker, in *The Age of Discontinuity*, has crystallized the new innovative technique in a graphic way. He calls it "a systematic organized leap into the unknown". Unlike the science of yesterday, he says, "it is not based on organizing our knowledge; it is based on organizing our ignorance". But amazingly these techniques are not taught in most schools, yet in many ways they are the key to the future.

Even worse: school tests are based on the principle that every question has one correct answer. The great breakthroughs in life come from entirely new answers. They come from challenging the status quo, not accepting it.

Courses in thinking should be a top priority in every school. Otherwise, as American educator Neil Postman has suggested in

Teaching As A Subversive Activity: children may "enter school as question marks but leave as periods".
California creative consultant Roger von Oech says, in *A Whack On The Side Of The Head*: "By the time the average person finishes college he or she will have taken over 2,600 tests, quizzes and exams. The 'right answer' approach becomes deeply ingrained in our thinking. This may be fine for some mathematical problems, where there is in fact only one right answer. The difficulty is that most of life isn't that way. Life is ambiguous; there are many right answers - all depending on what you are looking for. But if you think there is only one right answer, then you'll stop looking as soon as you find one." So how do you use your own brainpower to make Drucker's systematic organized leap into the unknown? These are the steps found to be most useful:

1. Define your problem

Define in advance your problem - specifically but not restrictively. Define your ideal solution and visualize it.
Define what you would like to achieve - ideally. And then organize your 100 billion active brain neurons to bridge the gap between where you are and where you want to be. It also helps greatly to visualize the ideal solution, to picture "in your mind's eye" the best possible result.

Let's use a world-famous industry as a typical model: the watch industry. Up to 1970, the entire industry was dominated by Switzerland. But its business model had not changed in half a century. By 1970 it was still making sales of $10 billion a year. But "by the early 1980s, most of that value had migrated away from the traditional Swiss business model to new business designs owned by Timex, Citizen, Seiko and Casio. Employment tumbled in parallel with the drop in value. From the mid-1970s to the early 1980s, the number of workers in the Swiss watch making industry contracted from 90,000 to 20,000."
So the industry called in consultant Nicolas Hayek. His experience in the industry: nil. But even as a boy "Hayek was always asking his family and teachers, 'Why do we do things the way we do?' He was born with an innate and incurable curiosity about the way things work and where we come from. He consumed every book he could find on physics, astronomy, the Big Bang, and Einstein's theories of mass and speed."
As an adult he applied that same curiosity to his newest challenge - and ended up reinventing an entire industry. Until he arrived on the

scene, most people bought a watch to last a lifetime. And those flocking to the new Japanese brands were also doing so because of their low cost. But Hayek started with a new series of questions: What did people want from a watch? Fun? Spirit? Style? Variety? Fashion? Those questions were to lead directly to the invention of the Swatch watch - not solely as a timekeeper but as an ever-changing fashion accessory. And with it, Hayek launched a marketing program to persuade customers to wear a different-colored watch with every dress or suit.

From 1983 to 1992, Swatch sold 100 million watches. By 1996 he had sold his 200 millionth.

Even the name itself emerged as typical of the innovation process. As Adrian J. Slywotzky and David J. Morrison recount in their excellent business book, *The Profit Zone:* "Hayek differentiated his watches by giving them a soul. He created a message, an emotional sense that appeals to everyone, conveying a sense of fun, of style, and of lightheartedness.

Then he wrapped it around indisputable high quality and low cost. All Hayek's new product lacked now was a name. 'We were working with an American advertising company,' Hayek says. 'We had the craziest names in the world and none pleased me. Finally, we went for lunch and this woman wrote on the blackboard "Swiss watch" and "second watch"' Then she wrote "Swatch". It helped that we were not very strong in English. We didn't know that "swatch" in English meant a cleaning towel. If we had known, we wouldn't have started the company with such a name!"' Problem defined. Vision set. And the two linked by new mixtures of old elements.

2. Gather all the facts

Since a great idea is a new combination of old elements, then the next step is to *gather all the facts* you can. Unless you know a big array of facts on any situation or problem, you're unlikely to hit on the perfect new solution.

Facts can be specific: those directly concerned with your job, industry or problem. And they can be general: the facts you gather from a thousand different sources. You will only be a great ideas-producer if you're a voracious seeker of information. Be a questioner, a reader, a challenger, and a gatherer of information, in notebooks and dendrites. There is no substitute for personalized, purposeful homework. What comes out must have gone in. The key is to somehow link information

filed in, say, "brain-cell number 369,124" on "dendrite 2,614", with another stored on "cell number 9,378,532" - or wherever.
Here your brain's patterning ability creates both problems and opportunities. Each one of us uses our brain for every waking minute to take action in a pre-patterned way - from walking to running, from reading to watching television, from driving a car to stopping at red lights. Your brain tends to store information in narrow channels, on associated "branches" for easy and quick retrieval, so we normally come up with the same answers.

3. Break the pattern

To solve problems creatively, however, you've got to open up new pathways, find new crossover points, and discover new linkages. You've got to break the pattern.
And the easiest way to do that is to start with questions that redirect your mind. What would happen to your problem if you doubled it, halved it, froze it, reconstituted it, reversed it, adapted it, rearranged it, and combined it with something else? What if you eliminated it - or part of it? What if you substituted one of the parts? If you made it smaller, shorter, lighter? Or you re-colored it, streamlined it, and magnified it? What if you repackaged it? Distributed it in a different way? What if you applied all your senses - and added scents or fragrances, added sounds or made it different to see or touch?

4. Go outside your own field

Try to put your existing preconceptions aside. The elements you use to solve problems should not only be those that are specific to the industry or process you're involved in. Use only those and you'll come up with the same old solutions.
Ask a teacher to redefine education, and generally he'll start thinking about school and not about interactive videodiscs or life in 2010. Ask your brain to add 1 plus 1 and it will automatically answer 2. It's programmed that way.
But your brain has also stored facts about thousands of different interests: from recipes to football. The answers to problems in farming may well come from meanderings in space research. All good inventors, innovators and creators develop an insatiable appetite for new knowledge. Always remember to ask.

5. Try various combinations

Next: since an idea is a new combination of old elements, try various combinations. Jot them down as they come to you. Try different starting points. Choose anything at random -a color, an animal, a country, an industry - and try to link it up with your problem and solution.

Work at it. Keep your notepad full. But a word of caution: don't concentrate too closely on your specific field or you'll be limited by your own preconceptions.

Read as widely as you can - particularly books on the future and challenging writings away from your own specialty. Keep asking: *What if?* "What if I combined this with that? What if I started from here instead of there?" And keep asking.

6. Use all your senses

It also helps greatly to consciously try to engage all your senses. If your problem has been defined mathematically, try to visualize some answers. Remember how Albert Einstein's theory of relativity came to him after he'd been daydreaming, imagining that he was travelling through space on a moonbeam.

Mind Mapping, too, is an excellent creative tool - to link information together in new ways, on new branches, in new clusters, so your ideas are not merely listed in one-dimensional lines.

Work at it until your head swims. Then . . .

7. Switch off - let it simmer

Like good food after you've eaten it, let your digestive juices take over and do the work - in this case the digestive juices of your own subconscious. Note the relaxation techniques we've touched on in accelerated learning, to put your brain into its most receptive and creative mode.

8. Sleep on it

Just before going to sleep at night, remind yourself of the problem - and the ideal solution. If you have a set deadline, feed that into your "brain-bank" too. And then your subconscious mind will take over. It never sleeps.

But as advertising leader David Ogilvy puts it: "You have to brief your subconscious. Then you have to switch off your thought processes and wait for something, for your subconscious to call you and say, 'Hey, I've got a good idea!' There are ways to do that. A lot of people find that to take a long hot bath produces good ideas. Other people prefer a long walk. I've always found that wine produces good ideas - the better the wine the better the idea." Eureka! It pops out.

The next step is the easiest of all: it pops out. You'll be shaving, or taking a shower, or sleeping - and suddenly the answer is there.
In part the process works because it's similar to the way your brain processes information in the first place. Just as you can use your subconscious to file information in patterns, so you can use your subconscious to deliberately break up those patterns and find new combinations. But, it only works if you state your vision and your goal specifically. It also pays to set a deadline, so your subconscious can feed that, too, into its data banks.

9. Recheck it

When the new answer has popped out, *recheck it*. Does it fully solve your problem? Can you amend it or improve it?
The system we've just highlighted could be called the problem-solving way to creativity.
An alternative is a vision or mission approach. That's the same as problem-solving - except you don't start with the problem. You start with a vision of a future where virtually every dream is now possible. Australian futurist Dr. Peter Ellyard is one of many who favor this approach. He feels that starting with a problem often limits the solution. "The dangers of a problem-centered approach can be best seen," he says, "in the inappropriately named 'health care' industry. In most first-world countries 'health care' is virtually out of control. The words 'health care' actually mean 'illness cure.' The industry consists of the activities of doctors, hospitals and pharmacies. The size of our health care budget has become an index of the nation's sickness, rather than its health. This forgets that the basic state of humans is to be healthy, not ill. We have adopted a problem-centered approach to health, largely defining health as an absence of illness, and a healthy future as an illness-free one. A *mission-directed* approach to promoting and maintaining health would be very different. It would concentrate on nutrition, exercise, good relationships, stress management and freedom from environmental contamination. This is a

totally different agenda. However, the current problem is that we now pour so much money and effort into the problem-centered, technology-driven approach that there are very few resources available for a mission-directed approach."

The current authors certainly wouldn't disagree with this analysis - except to say that the "problem" was not correctly defined. And Ellyard makes a vital point: generally we all try to define a problem too narrowly. Define your problem as "unemployment", for example, and you may restrict your answers to new jobs - and not consider retraining leave or the desirability of leisure and study-time.

When consulting engineer William J. J. Gordon was given the task of finding a new way to open cans, he deliberately didn't use the word "can-opener" when briefing his engineers and designers. Instead they toyed with such notions as a banana and its easy-peel abilities. Their eventual solution: the ring-pulls you now see on most tear-tab cans. A "can-opener" approach would have limited the result.

Whether you use the problem-solving or mission-directed approach, you generally won't come up with a great idea unless you define a specific goal in advance.

There are, of course, many exceptions. Bacteriologist Alexander Fleming stumbled on penicillin when confronted with a strange mould growing at St. Mary's Hospital in London.

And when Massachusetts's inventor Percy Spencer was working on a novel radar system in 1945, it struck him that the radiation it emitted could have a culinary use. So he hung a pork chop in front of the magnetron machine he was working on. And, as British BBC presenters Peter Evans and Geoff Deehan report, he "produced the first microwave meal in history".In another of history's quirks, it was the Japanese who capitalized on the invention. "When a Japanese firm started to manufacture magnetrons, it was forbidden under the peace treaty to undertake military contracts. Therefore it concentrated on peaceful uses of microwave technology; now Japan leads the world in microwave sales." Or at least it did until the Koreans caught up.

But most breakthroughs come from a firm vision of the future: a specific goal. Many of those creative techniques can be adapted from other fields. Advertising, for example, has given us "brainstorming"- the original idea of Alex Osborn, one of the founders of Batten, Barton, Durstine and Osborn, the giant advertising agency.

Here are some specific examples of how you can apply the brainstorming, ideas-creation process in practice:

When you're looking for a new idea, can you:
Double it: like London's double-decker buses? *Halve it:* like bikinis

We suspect that overwhelmingly it is because of the way schools and curricula are structured. *From the very moment of starting school, most children are taught that the answers have already been found.* Even more: they are taught that success is learning a limited range of those answers - absorbed from a teacher - and feeding them back correctly at exam time. Yet that is not the way the real world innovates. The simple questions on the past three pages are typical of the queries posed in businesses every day as they strive to do things "better, faster, and cheaper".

Don Koberg and Jim Bagnall, in their book *The Universal Traveller*, have suggested other words to encourage innovation: multiply, divide, eliminate, subdue, invert, separate, transpose, unify, distort, rotate, flatten, squeeze, complement, submerge, freeze, soften, fluff-up, bypass, add, subtract, lighten, repeat, thicken, stretch, extrude, repel, protect, segregate, integrate, symbolize, abstract and dissect.

Stanford University engineer James Adams suggests thinking up your own favorite "bug list" - the things that irritate you - to start you thinking. And he lists among his own: corks that break off in wine bottles, vending machines that take your money with no return, bumper stickers that cannot be removed, crooked billiard cue sticks, paperless toilets, dripping faucets and "one sock". "If you run out of bugs before ten minutes," says Adams, "you are either suffering from a perceptual or emotional block or have life unusually under control."

Another technique is to focus on 1,000 percent breakthroughs. What can you do ten times faster, better, cheaper? What is the "killer application" in your field: the big "Aha!" that can take your company, your school or your industry to new peaks of excellence? That's what Microsoft has achieved in computer software; what Netscape has done in Internet browsers; what Canon has achieved in color copiers.

Given the tremendous increase in technology, in almost any field 1,000 per cent improvements are possible: in some operations. Learning to typeset magazine advertisements and newspapers, for instance, once took a six-year apprenticeship. To "makeup" pages took five years of training. Today, with desktop computerized publishing, any competent typist can compress much of that 11-year training into a week. What would it take to achieve similar breakthroughs in your field?

At the other extreme, if you learn only one word of Japanese in your life, make it Kaizen. It means continuous improvement. But it means much more than that. It means a philosophy that encourages every person in an industry - every day - to come up with suggestions for improving everything: themselves, their job, their lunchroom, their office layout, their telephone answering habits and their products. Says Toyota Motor chairman Eiji Toyoda: "One of the features of the Japanese workers is that they use their brains as well as their hands. Our workers provide 1.5 million suggestions a year, and 95 per cent of them are put to practical use." And at Nissan Motors "any suggestion that saves at least 0.6 seconds - the time it takes a worker to stretch out his hand or walk half a step - is seriously considered by management." Matsushita, the giant Japanese electronics company, receives about 6.5 million ideas every year from its staff. And the big majority is put into operation quickly.

It is beyond the scope of this book to cover the total secret of Japan's Total Quality Management and Kaizen movements. But to test, in part, the effectiveness of their method, try an introductory *Kaizen* on anything you're involved in. One excellent method is to use David Buffin's hexagon *Think Kit*. Staff or students are encouraged to fire in new ideas. The teacher or facilitator writes each on a colored hexagon and attaches the hexagons to a large magnetic board. The group then arranges the hexagons around various themes or activities, and agrees on the main priorities. These are then left on display as a continual spur to agreed action.

For business we prefer to marry the two methods together: to look for the big *Aha!* Idea for strategic planning (what is the really big breakthrough that will change the future of your company or industry?) and *Kaizen* (how can you involve all your staff in continuously striving to upgrade every aspect of that performance?). In oversimplified terms, many would describe *Aha!* As the key to American business success, and *Kaizen* as the Japanese secret weapon. Their "marriage" is *The Third Way*. And an excellent way to display them is on another David Buffin innovation, the arrowed action kit (see illustration next page): again a good permanent and colorful visible reminder of agreed goals and actions.

Many universities, of course, would say they have always taught thinking as part of logic, psychology and philosophy. But most schools don't teach what Edward de Bono has termed *lateral thinking*: the ability to open-mindedly; search for new ideas, look in new directions. Roger von Oech thinks even the terms logical and lateral thinking are too restrictive. He says we're also capable of conceptual thinking, analytical thinking, speculative thinking, right-brain thinking, critical thinking, foolish thinking, convergent thinking, weird thinking, reflective thinking, visual thinking, symbolic thinking, propositional thinking, digital thinking, metaphorical thinking, mythical thinking, poetic thinking, nonverbal thinking, elliptical thinking, analogical thinking, lyrical thinking, practical thinking, divergent thinking, ambiguous thinking, constructive thinking, thinking about thinking, surreal thinking, focused thinking, concrete thinking and fantasy thinking.

But most people unwittingly limit their thinking potential. One reason is the brain's ability to file material inside existing patterns. When a new problem is tackled, we're conditioned to go down the track of previous answers. We all have preconceptions, taboos and prejudices, though few of us ever admit to them. They can be emotional, cultural, religious, educational, national, psychological, sexual or culinary.

We are also preconditioned from school to come up with "the right answer" - not the open-minded challenge for a better way. Almost every adult who has succeeded at high school or college will have firm ideas on the best educational system. And it will generally be the system that he succeeded in. Listen to anyone praise a "good school" and you will almost certainly find a school that suits that particular person's learning style.

Now that's not unusual. You could probably go through life and never find a person totally objective about everything. And fortunately no one system of education, or religion, or health, suits all. So perhaps the first step in "conceptual blockbusting" - to use James Adams' term - is to accept that we all have fears, we all have biases. The best way we know to start overcoming them is to combine fun and humor. That often works for students in particular. A fun-filled atmosphere can lead to high creativity.

If you're not used to "far-out" brainstorming sessions, probably a good warm-up exercise is to start with a humorous challenge. Try inventing a new golf ball - one that can't get lost. Or planning what you'd do with a holiday on the moon or underwater. Or ask some "What if?" questions. What if computers ran the government? Then use some of de Bono's techniques, such as PMI, CAF, C&S, APC and his "Six Thinking Hats."

PMI standards for Plus, Minus and Interesting. Here the students are asked to choose a fairly outlandish statement, and in three columns write down all the points they can think of to be "plus" factors, then all the "minuses," and lastly all the reasons the proposition could be "interesting."

CAF means Consider All Factors. And again write them down, searching for new factors that don't spring immediately to mind.

C & S stands for Consequences and Sequel. Logically, both should be listed under CAF, but de Bono says that most people just do not consider all the consequences unless their attention is specifically drawn to them.

APC stands for Alternatives, Possibilities and Choices. And again the reasons are obvious: a list that encourages you to speculate.

As de Bono summarizes one of his other techniques: "The theme of my book *Six Thinking Hats* is simple. There is the white hat for neutral facts, figures and information. There is the red hat to allow a person to put forward feelings, hunches and intuitions - without any need to justify them. The black hat is for the logical negative, and the yellow hat for the logical positive. For creativity there is the green hat. The blue hat is the control hat, and looks at the thinking itself rather than at the subject - like an orchestra conductor controlling the orchestra. The purpose is to provide a means for rapidly switching thinkers from one mode to another - without causing offence."

All are excellent classroom techniques. Especially the "six hats" - when you go to the trouble to obtain some bizarre models, in colors and odd shapes, and pass them around so each person can act the part. But the simple ideas we have suggested earlier in this chapter are the ones we have found to work effectively in virtually any situation: in advertising, business, marketing, selling, exporting, market research and all aspects of learning and education. They work, we believe, because they show the logical links between sequential and creative thinking. Your critical "left-brain" logic sees the common sense in the step-by-step link-up to the "right-brain's" creative ability.

They start, of course, by tapping into the outstanding power of the brain. And the brain's potential, as we'll turn to next, is grounded in processing which goes back to the start of life - even before birth itself.

IV) Transforming Creativity into Business Reality

Have you ever thought about using an umbrella that's strapped to your dog and allows you to take your dog for a walk in the rain? I'll bet you've never seen one? Or how about a device that allows a baby to drink his or her bottle while sitting in a baby seat, allowing her mom to have her hands free? How about a totally redesigned shopping cart, made with a lightweight plastic design, with compartments to hold your produce, meats, and dry goods in separate areas? Or an aquatic-treadmill, that combines the use of a pool and treadmill combination to allow for aging baby boomers to relax sore joints and muscles?

These are but a handful of ideas that come to mind when you begin to think about how to apply the creativity process.

The innovation process when broken down to a formula is really composed of five major areas: Research, Ideation, Evaluation & Alignment, Validation and Launch. Let's explore these in a little more detail.

<u>Research</u> is the process of understanding the market, the customer, product and process. It's also observing the market and real world situations to validate the need for a product or service in the marketplace. I have found the best resources for research are often the most simple: newspaper and magazine articles, using everyday devices in your home and determine where gaps in usage might be. Another source of doing research is watching children. Children are great at improvising new ways of doing things, as they have no pre-conceived notions of how things should be done. They are a great source of observing how to innovate a new way of doing something. Another method of research is observing people at the park, shopping mall, pumping gas and going to the bank to use an ATM machine. Observation of people's actions and how they interact with their surroundings is another great way to determine how to innovate new products and services.

My example earlier regarding the dog umbrella was based on that very observation of watching a young woman walking her dog in our neighborhood without rain protection. This form of research is very effective as it allows you to view in real-time the gaps or needs in societies that aren't being fulfilled.

<u>Idea Generation</u> is the process of visualizing new concepts and non-traditional ways of solving a problem, looking at the problem or gap in an upside down fashion. You have to come out of your typical ways of looking at things and understand the world can always use a better mousetrap. You have to train your mind to think and behave differently. What are some of the ways you view current products and or services that can be enhanced, provide a better service or allow for more than one use. Remember what we talked about in the first

chapter about recombining similar elements to in effect make something better, cheaper, and faster. My vision of this process is to have Idea Generation Centers where potential entrepreneurs could go and work through these 5-step processes and trial their ideas with their peers.

<u>Market Evaluation & Alignment</u> is building and testing the prototypes, analyze the financial model, review with the customer and refine your design. Once your evaluation is completed and your research is founded on solid evidence, it's time to build and test your prototype. This process isn't necessarily reserved for physical products as it can be used for service level offerings as well. You'll want to take samples of your product or service and test it in the marketplace within a sampling of your targeted market. Be mindful to record your data and capture responses from your test market. These will be vital as you add improvements and refinements to your end product or service. You'll want to also make sure at this stage that you have evaluated and incorporated all of your costs into the product as well and that you've built in a profit margin. You'll find below a listing of many basic human needs that can help you determine how your business can fulfill a trend in the marketplace.

- **Acknowledgement**
- **Adventure**
- **Beauty**
- **Challenge**
- **Control**
- **Education**
- **Fitness**
- **Food**
- **Freedom**
- **Friendship**
- **Health**
- **Hygiene**
- **Independence**
- **Information**
- **Knowledge**
- **Leisure**
- **Love**
- **Money**

Power
Privacy
Protection / Shelter
Relaxation
Security
Self esteem
Sleep
Stability
Status
Time
Water

The quality must be beyond question:
This is always the first rule of any business. Good products have a way of selling themselves. Bad ones will make you wish you still had a day job. There's no compromise here. Get this one right before you do anything else.

It must be unique:
Or it should at least be presented in a unique way. Many new products and or services are typically similar but with a different spin on an existing idea.

There should be an EXISTING demand for the product or service:
Small business owners often make the mistake of trying to create a demand for a new product. The simple truth is that creating a demand for your product is very, very expensive - that's why companies like Coca-Cola can do it and you can't. They have millions to spend on marketing. For a small business you should focus on satisfying existing demands.

It must be user-friendly:
Off the top of my head, I can think of two really **fantastic** Internet products that never achieved commercial success because getting them to work was a nightmare. Don't expect the customer to download any additional software or plug-ins to get the thing to work. They won't.

It must be legal:
Remember that the Internet is international. Is your product legal and safe everywhere? There's no need to go read up on the commercial laws of every country in the world. Just create a straightforward, original, honest product and you'll be safe.

It has to be credible:
If you're a well-established company with a proven track record, skip this step. If you're not, develop a product that can incorporate an evaluation version. If it's a book, give the table of contents and chapter 1 away for free. If it's software, offer a time-limited trial etc.

It should support repeat-business
This is not really a MUST, but it's a big plus if you can add it. A large part of success lies in your base of faithful **repeat** buyers. Quality comes into play again. Consumers will pay you over and over again if they know they are getting quality and value for their purchase. Remember, it is more difficult to create brand new customers versus continually satisfying your existing customer base. Repeat business is pure gold.

Validation

Conduct Marketing trials, Perform Customer Trials, Confirm Economics: You want to make sure these are happening simultaneously. As an example, as you conduct your marketing trials and accumulate the data this information has to re-circulate into the Customer Trials so that updated marketing information is captured and updated. This also coincides with the financial and economics to make sure you are not exceeding costs and that costs are still in line with what you will charge, profit margin and revenue targets. This process of validation might continue as a revolving loop for a while as the bugs and kinks are worked out. This phase contains a lot of trial and error. This validation stage is critical as it allows you to continually refine your data and marketing findings. The results will be advantageous, as you will produce a product or service that has stood the test of the marketing trials.

Product/Service Launch

The next step is the day of reckoning as I like to call it. This is the day you launch your product to the marketplace. All the research, idea creation, and marketing validation come together and you are now ready to serve the public. However, it doesn't stop here. You will need to constantly refine and monitor your product or service in the marketplace. Just because your product does well at the launch does not mean you can put it on auto-pilot. Any great product (think Microsoft) will need to be constantly upgraded and enhanced to meet the growing demands of the marketplace. Many great products have been launched at their inception, only to see them fade away over time. Truly great products stand the test of time because they are re-marketed, re-branded and re-launched!

V) Trends in the Marketplace

A crucial component to starting any business big or small is to look at current and future trends in the marketplace. In this chapter we will look at trends occurring in business, education, personal services, leisure, technology, financial and population trends. It's extremely important to look at these trends, as they are a prime indicator of what demand will look like in the future. Trends are not to be confused with a fad, which is something that is shorter versus a trend, which is based on a more long-term impact.

As the U.S. economy moved from agriculture to industry, thousands of industries began to emerge throughout the United States. Workers began to move from the farmlands to the inner cities to take advantage of these newly created jobs. With this trend came the need for the automobile, apartment houses, small businesses such as cleaners, local markets and such that provided services to this growing inner city population. Many entrepreneurs saw this trend and began to set up shop in the burgeoning city developments. As more people migrated from the farmlands, the need for small businesses grew to meet this demand.

Trend spotting is probably the single most important aspect of how to spot opportunity in the marketplace. There are literally thousands of examples of how tracking trends can help in developing the insight to create a business opportunity. The single largest example that comes to mind is the baby boomer generation. There are 76 million of them in total. These were the men and women born between 1946 through 1962. This segment of the population of the market has been analyzed, marketed to, researched and sold to over the last fifty plus years. And why, they represent tremendous buying power! From everything to baby food, toothpaste, chef boy-are-dee, Rolling Stones tickets and the list goes on and on. Companies like Campbell's Soup, P&G, Coca-Cola, and Colgate-Palmolive built huge marketing programs around marketing to this huge American demographic. Companies were built around this generation. A generation of music cultural icons: Bob Dylan, Rolling Stones, The Who, and The Beatles sold millions of records and concert tickets to this generation. The baby boomer generation bought millions of homes, cars, stocks, motorcycles and gadgets during the last 50 years creating an economic tsunami in the marketplace! And they continue to do so.

It's estimated that as these baby boomers retire, they will become the wealthiest generations of Americans to retire in history, with more disposable income than their predecessors. They will continue to buy vacation homes, health and beauty aids, financial planning services, prescription drugs, and exercise equipment, gifts for grandchildren well into the next 15-20 years. Think about that for a moment and the potential opportunity it presents. If you are able to provide a good or a service directly related to this generational buying power, you would have created a lasting source of income for decades to come not only for yourself, but also for your children and your heirs, allowing them to be free from the overwhelming uncertainly of finding and keeping a job in today's volatile marketplace. This is exactly what I am talking about when I stress how we need to be idea generators and creators of value that provide a service or product that appeals to a mass market. What better mass market than the baby boomer generation! Other trends in the marketplace can be found in abundance in other areas. Think of the do-it-yourself explosion that took place over the last 15 years. Homeowners, tired of hiring an expert over the last several years and paying high fees decided to take on many projects themselves allowing for the rise in such big box retailers such as Home Depot and Lowe's. These organizations thrive on this do-it-yourself mentality. They exist because of a trend in the marketplace for homeowner's to tackle projects on their own. Another example is the use of personal computers in your home and in the workplace. This trend of using pc's has created an incredible profitable industry in software, from desktop publishing to turbo tax and will maker to name a few. Again, the pattern is following and tracking a trend and as it develops building a business that services that trend profitably. EBay, the online auction site built its business model around individuals who wanted to trade collectibles and other valuables in an on-line setting where buyers and sellers come together in an electronic marketplace. The response is overwhelming and users and subscribers continue to flock to the web-site to buy and sell good and services. Small businesses are developed around this business model and entrepreneurs continue to find ways to start small businesses using eBay as their business framework. I see this trend continuing to grow as more consumers embrace the Internet and have a global marketplace at the stroke of a keyboard.

Along with the trend of the aging baby boomers there will come a change in the demographic landscape. The nation's population will rise 49% to 420 million by 2050, and Americans who are white, but not Hispanic, will make up only half the total, according to projections by the Census Bureau. These projections suggest that whites that are not Hispanic – the dominant population group since the nation was founded in 1776 – will see their share of population drop from 69% in 2000 to 50% in 2050. In 1950, the share was 90%. The 50-year outlook paints a picture of an aging population in a country that will continue to grapple with increasing racial and ethnic diversity. Hispanic and Asian populations are expected to triple. The oldest baby boomers will turn 65 in 2011. By 2030, 20% of Americans will be 65 or older. That's up from 12% in 2000. This profound demographic shift promises to redefine American society at every level – from the ethnic make-up of suburban neighborhoods to public education, elderly care and voting patterns.

Economists say that as the U.S. population ages, an increase in the working-age population could help pay for Social Security, Medicare and other benefits for seniors. The population increase also will fuel the housing market. Federal Reserve Chairman Alan Greenspan has cited the increase in the population for helping to keep the housing industry humming during the last several years. While far lower than the 87% population increase from 1950 to 2000, the projected 49% growth by 2050 contrasts sharply with forecasts for most European countries. Germany and Italy are on the brink of population declines because of low birth rates. Hispanics surpassed blacks as the largest minority group in 2002, when their numbers hit 38.8 million. The number of Hispanics is expected to increase by 2050 to 103 million. Their share of the nation's population will almost double to 24%.

Keep in mind the census numbers are projections - not predictions. They're based on current immigration policy or spikes in the death rate caused by wars or epidemics could significantly alter the figures. In 1940, for example, no one predicted the post-war baby boom that began in 1946 and lasted to 1964. The Census projections also don't take into account the growing number of racial intermarriages that continue to blur racial and ethnic identity. What projections generally do is assume that Hispanic women have Hispanic children and those children have Hispanic children and so on.

You can look at trends as a developing market opportunity that allows you to create a business around a growing need in the marketplace. The difference, typically, between a trend and a fad is that a trend is something that will be around for a greater length of time. You can apply a business model to literally thousands of trends in the marketplace. Remember the boom in healthy lifestyle living during the 1980's That spurned a tremendous need for businesses to satisfy the trend: work-out gyms, work-out tapes, healthier choices in fast-food establishments and an increase in sports activities such as running, golf, tennis and other lifestyle sports. Another example is women who re-entered the workforce during the 1980's as well. Once women went back into the workforce, the need for daycare businesses began to spring up across the country in droves. Who will take care of all these children once all these moms went back to work?

How about the trend in corporate downsizing? The business response to this has been the need for temporary agencies. Businesses are constantly shedding the burden of full-time workers and leveraging the use of temp workers. There are literally thousands of temp agencies that dot the American landscape. In conjunction with this trend is the need to evaluate which jobs can or cannot be outsourced. A need will arise for companies to effectively review and understand how they make the decisions to outsource or not. A business model that leverages this business activity can do quite well as the trend will continue to outsource jobs that are routine in nature.

And let's not forget about a current trend surrounding consumers desire to amass a huge amount of debt during this period of low interest rates. With interest rates being the lowest in 46 years, consumers are re-financing their mortgages, lines of credit, new cars, etc. What happens when interest rates begin to rise and people are stuck with loans they can't pay because they are highly leveraged? It will become quickly apparent they will need some sort of credit counseling and financial planning services as they will be looking for ways to climb out of debt and restore their credit and avoid bankruptcy. This need in the marketplace will certainly create the need for businesses to serve this area of financial services. If you have a background in credit counseling, accounting, taxes, debt restructuring and financial planning, this could certainly be a lucrative area for you.

If you refer back to several paragraphs on the changing demographic landscape, one can ascertain many different trends to emerge from this change in the population. If you think about the growing Hispanic population, what does that tell you? What can you ascertain from this trend? How about the need for education on American Business practices to the Hispanic community who want to learn how to operate a small business in the U.S? How about language and writing courses to help them to become as fluent as possible in our language and communication?

What about their desire for clothing, food, newspapers, etc, that caters to their wants and needs as a demographic?

Remember, the key points in this section of the book are to literally create a connection between a trend in the marketplace and a business model. By linking these two together, with careful research, idea generation and execution you have the recipe for a successful business opportunity for years to come. Some trends have been in existence for sometime and some are just beginning to emerge. We can see as the aging population of the baby boomers and the increased length of years that baby boomers live will create tremendous demands on society to care for older Americans. As more Americans are living longer and staying healthy, they will desire to stay in their own homes and refuse to live in retirement centers. A trend and business opportunities will begin to develop to serve the needs of these people such as companionship, transportation, and house cleaning as well as cooking and paying the bills. Many times, families of these older Americans do not live close by and will require outside assistance for non-medical care. Family members who live away will pay a certified agency to take care of many of these tasks for their aging parents. There are several franchise opportunities that have cropped up in the last several years that cater to this very need. Remember, as this trend continues, a business model can be created around this need and ultimately provide a source of income.

The important thing to remember about capitalizing on a trend is that it will create "natural demand". What I mean by this is that a trend will be a force that will automatically create demands in the marketplace through the normal process of capitalism. By following a trend with a business model, you are creating a service or product to satisfy a growing demand in the marketplace. Many would-be business creators get caught up in this trap of falling in love so much with their product or service they forget that you have to also have the demand and the desire in the marketplace to move your product or service from concept to reality.

There have been many entrepreneurs who have failed with this concept and not made any money because they didn't properly research or test market their idea to see if demand existed. By accurately looking at the market and doing the right level of research and test marketing the product or service, you can save countless hours of frustration and dollars!

VI) 21st Century Business Opportunities

I'd like to spend some time getting a bit more specific about which opportunities will be the best one's to pursue in the 21st century, based on current and future trends. This section will tie together emerging trends and how they translate to viable business opportunities. I've spent a lot of time researching this section and I wanted to make sure the research conducted gave you the most comprehensive list of opportunities and not just a re-hashing of the same old buzzwords you've all heard before. We looked at many different areas: lifestyle trends, technology, the aging baby boomers, security, dining out/tastes in food, the teen market, vacation trends and a lot more.

We wanted to make sure you had a cross-section of areas to choose from and that you could make your choices based on your personal preferences and were you saw the best fit for yourself. I also wanted to make sure that my readers did understand the great need to be able to think and act for ourselves in this new 21st Century Marketplace and that the days of big companies taking care of us and the security they used to provide are gone and will not return. We must take action and draw on our experiences, skills and creativity to forge to ways a building businesses and creating a livelihood for our families and ourselves. We need to teach these lessons to our children as well. Not that it was anyone's fault when I was growing up, but no one ever told me or exposed me to the possibilities of starting something on my own, to create and to develop a business from the ground floor. These weren't things that were talked about in school or in my home. But what if they were!

What if I was immersed in these discussions in school or home? What if my parents discussed the benefits of being independent in my thinking about starting something on my own? What if there were a school curriculum that was focused on finding the right business opportunity that capitalized on your abilities and creativity or that centered on investing in assets such as real estate and not liabilities. If, If, If!!! My point is it's not too late! We as parents have the ability, no the duty, to tell and explain to our children the benefits of using their talents to create and develop new businesses from scratch! My point is that to get children to understand, to really understand, they must be exposed to the possibilities at a young age! They need to hear it in their everyday lives, as much as possible.

Remember, our children will inherit a different world from the one you and I grew up in. Many of the paradigms we've come to know and expect about going to school, getting good grades and getting a job just don't hold true anymore. You see it in the headlines everyday! With the latest headline being the off shoring of U.S. jobs. About 15 years ago is was all about blue-collar and manufacturing jobs going overseas, to Singapore, China and Korea, now the trend is shifting toward white-collar jobs, particularly in information technology. Most jobs today that are routine or one's that can be broken down into routine activities will certainly be vulnerable to off-shoring. And trust me, organizations today, whether its government, business, or other will constantly be looking to see how jobs can be down-sized, eliminated or off-shored to other countries.

Let's now take a look at some of the areas that will be in what I consider the "growth quadrant". These are business opportunities that I believe will tie closely to a particular trend in the marketplace. In many instances they will not be expensive to start up and many can be started from your own home, reducing the need for office space, rent and other costs associated with an office location. As you work through each of these business possibilities, keep in mind you are looking for one that will play to your strengths. We all have weaknesses that we need to improve, however, if you view this selection and pick one that leverages your strengths you will be in a much better position for success. Picking and choosing an area because you think it will make a ton of money or offer prestige are not the right reasons to pick a business. You have to pick it because you know you will enjoy going to work everyday. Now granted, there will be things about the job you won't like, won't like doing and quite frankly, might want someone else to do. However, you should feel comfortable about the day-to-day operations of running the business.

I've captured each business opportunity (50 in total) below and will explain why these businesses make sense, how you can get started and where you can operate.

Let's begin, shall we:

Major Trends in the 21st Century Marketplace

Trend #1 - Business Outsourcing

What's driving this trend?

This is a good time to be in the outsourcing/staffing industry. In the first quarter of 2006, U.S. sales of outsourcing/temporary and contract staffing services rose 5 percent, to $13.1 billion, according to the American Staffing Association (ASA). That marked the third consecutive quarter of growth after six straight declining quarters.

This type of service business should come as no surprise to anyone as the demand for temporary workers continues to grow, and companies become increasingly reluctant to bring on full-time workers because of the huge burden of employee expenses. Hiring temporary workers allows companies to hire workers and not be burdened with the high cost of salaries and benefits. Employee and labor costs continue to be the most expensive items on a company's balance sheet. Temporary workers give companies all the benefit and minimal risk. This trend, I believe, is one that will be here for many years. As we entered 2007, there continues to be a strong desire for temporary agencies; one area for temporary services that will grow significantly is for healthcare professionals. This trend ties in closely with the demand overall for the rising need for more healthcare jobs in nursing, nurses aides, and non-medical in-home care. Another area in particular that will experience growth for temporary workers is small business. Most small businesses starting out today don't have a huge payroll to staff all areas and all departments. They are very selective on which positions they want to fill and where they will get the most value. Many small companies will actually hire "part-time" CEO's or CFO's on a consulting basis and not hire them on a full time basis. Their contract may go out as far as 6-months or a year or more. And these CEO's or CFO's don't worry about getting full time work as they do this as a consulting career. They will finish one assignment with a small company and then move on to the next one. The small company benefits as they get a "C" level professional that they can leverage their experience and skills and not be burdened with a huge salary and benefits costs. The trend today in both large and small businesses is to reduce costs, particularly in human resources. Hiring someone brand new for an organization is one of the biggest costs a company can incur. Training, salary, benefits and retention costs are a huge expense on a company's books and if they can avoid hiring full time people, they will do so.

I mentioned earlier the need for temporary healthcare workers earlier in the chapter. As the demand for health care professionals grows, the need for temporary workers will grow as well. If you have a background in this field, you are already a bit ahead of the game. Knowing and understanding the profession and specific job skills will help you better understand how to serve this market.

What skills are required?

It will help greatly if you've been involved in the temporary services business. Knowing the business side of how to own and operate this business will be extremely helpful. It's important to know, if you've had this experience, what will differentiate you from the competition. Why will customers want to use your service over others in the same business? You will also need great communication and interpersonal skills. This is a business that requires good sales and marketing acumen. Clients are buying a service from you and they will want to be reassured they can establish a relationship with you over a period of time. They will need to trust you and that you will provide them with the right level of resources as they grow their businesses. Your communication and people skills will be required throughout your business relationship with your customers.

This is a huge and growing market and you will also need to have a good sense of marketing acumen. Your greatest asset will be your ability to create excitement and interest in your service. Selling them on your great temporary business and all it has to offer will create a marketing buzz that will circulate throughout the community. If you are confident that you have the right marketing skills, then you are off to a good start. If not, don't hesitate to spend the money on a good marketing consultant. You'll be glad you did. Due to the fact this is a huge market, you will need to carve out a market niche. The healthcare area is good place to start since the need for both full time and temporary workers will explode over the next several decades.

Another area of special interest might be information or knowledge workers. Many companies are looking to hire these types of workers on a temporary basis. Companies looking to mine marketing data and others types of information from the web hire information workers to do this research and then report back to the company with their findings. Starting a temp agency that places these types of workers that have this experience is a good way to create a service that others currently are not doing.

What are my start- up requirements?

This certainly a business you can start from home, however, you will need an area (office) to conduct interviews and meet with potential customers and contractors. As the business grows you may want to keep this mind. If you have worked in this business before, it will help to bring that knowledge and experience to your own start up. That will be a major start up requirement, if you have it to bring at the start. If not, not a major problem, you'll just have to spend some time building and marketing the business to gain traction and get customers signed up for your service. The key to success is to make sure you hire contractors that have a good solid track record in the temp field. Your reputation depends on it and the more time you invest up front and making sure you have good candidates, the better off your business will be in the long run. Make sure you also look into the legal and financial components of hiring temporary workers or contractors for your service. There are certain accounting requirements that you and the contractors should know about before you bring them on. And I'll say this in most of my start up requirements section; please invest in a good quality desktop computer. One that can handle the data and storage needs of your business. At least 512M and 200GB of hard drive will get you off to a fine start. I also recommend some start-up capital. You'll need to estimate how much money you'll need to invest in the business before you start breaking even and having the business paying for itself. I would estimate to have at least 6 months to a year in reserves of cash so you can fund the initial start up of the business. It will help to do this initially so that you aren't crunched for cash or asking for loans from banks and relatives. Don't put yourself in that position. Go ahead and plan for it from the start.

At last but not least, please do your homework and research on the legal, tax and financial ramifications of starting a business of this type. Talk to SCORE (Small Business Advisors on Starting a Small

Business), you can access this group through your local SBA-Small Business Administration. It's better to be over prepared that under prepared!

Check out these additional resources to learn more about the temporary services trends:

Web-sites:

www.vedior.com

www.poolia.com

www.doing-business.info
www.outsourcetoindia.com
www.offshorexperts.com
www.newwork.com
www.chillibreeze.com
www.phptr.com

Books:

Start Your Own Staffing Service, by Krista Thoren Turner

Strategic Outsourcing, by Maurice F. Greaver
Outsourcing America, by Ron Hira, Anil Hira
Intelligent IT Outsourcing, by Sara Cullen, Leslie Willcocks

Best Businesses to start based on this trend:

Temporary Services Agency specializing in niche services, i.e. medical, healthcare, Armed Services Veterans

Advisor to large companies

Author/Writer on Temporary Services Trends

Outsourcing Consulting Firm
Niche Outsourcing Firm for specific industries
Industry Expert
Writer/Publisher on Outsourcing Industry

Trend#2- Entrepreneurism & Small Business Ownership

What's driving this trend?

Small business start-ups will accelerate as more baby boomers enter their post-working years and begin to explore opportunities in entrepreneurship. Many of them will realize they are unable to find a new job and in particular, they won't be able to replace their former salaries. Most will become disenchanted with a job search that used to take months and is now taking years. This frustration will begin to transform itself into a level of fierce independence. Many people fifty and over will eventually stop looking for a traditional job and begin to look at the possibilities of starting something on their own. They will come to the realization they have many good years to work and be productive and the thought of going back to work for someone else will hold little appeal. The dream of starting an enterprise on their own and making it successful will become irresistible. It may have been a dream of theirs for years, but they decided not to act upon it because of all the other obligations that life brought. Now, many of those obligations have disappeared. Their children are grown and gone and on their own, the house is paid for and their financial picture looks much brighter.

The notion of starting a small enterprise suddenly holds some promise. They've worked hard their whole lives for someone else and they've come to the conclusion that it's now time to invest in their passion. Many will need help in the form of information, business training, and financing as well as idea generation. People who have worked for someone their entire careers will need a lot of help and support to get started. That's why I think small business incubation centers have a strong future. First off, rents have become much cheaper over the last decade as commercial buildings were over built in the late 1990's and many buildings are vacant or not at full capacity. If you are considering this type of business, you should be able to negotiate some good rates on renting or leasing a building depending upon the region you live in. Being able to negotiate good rates and to lock in for long term will help lower your overall cost.

Also, the track record for businesses that use an incubator is actually very good. A 1997 statistic shows that 87% of incubator graduate businesses are still in business five years later. Using an incubator in your start up phase allows a small, fledgling business to grow unfettered and to use shared resources and equipment at a fraction of what it would cost them if they were to buy it separately on their own. A good resource for researching incubation services is the NBIA (National Business Incubation Association) Using an incubation service also makes a small company look big as it has many of the amenities of a big business; office location, shared equipment, administrative assistant and many of the high-tech computer systems that big companies enjoy.

Using an incubation service also allows your customers to connect with other small business people. It allows for knowledge sharing and support among people who are in a similar situation. It's difficult to put a price tag on the benefits of information sharing!

There are really three main approaches you can take when looking to start your own business: start a new business from the ground up, buy an existing business, or buy a franchise. All three have their advantages and disadvantages. If you are a creative innovator and like to build or develop something from inception to final completion, starting a brand new business may be the way to go. If however, you want to mitigate your risk and get involved in an on-going established business, then buying an existing business may be right for you. And then there is the last category of buying a franchise. A franchise opportunity is great for someone who wants to buy a proven method for an established business. All the product development, marketing, pricing and distribution for a franchise business have already been designed by the franchisor. It helps to eliminate a lot of the trial and error effort a new business owner has to go through before they have a proven business model. I would suggest that you carefully examine each model and determine which one works the best for you, your family and your financial situation.

What skills are required?

What I like about this business opportunity is that many of the skills you acquired while working for larger more established company are transferable here as well. Small companies, like their counterparts need help and consulting with marketing, finances, sales and manufacturing to name a few. So, if you've spent the majority of working life in these areas, you can transfer this knowledge in helping smaller businesses get started.

Many small businesses would welcome this help as they value an objective outside opinion, particularly if you are bringing other experiences from other small-businesses as well. The power of knowledge is the key. If you decide to pursue this type of business, it probably will be helpful to establish yourself in a particular area of strength and bring others into your businesses that have complimentary skills. For instance, your experience might be in marketing; however, you might not be versed in finance and accounting. Bringing on people who have other skills can only strengthen your bench and give potential customers the security that you have a well-rounded team that can satisfy many needs. It helps to promote a "one-stop shop" where your clients only have to go to one source (you) for their business needs. This is critical because if they have to go to multiple places for services, they may not see value in using your firm. Make sure you consider having a well-rounded staff when developing your own business plan. I have a good friend who works in this field, but he takes a different approach to providing a service. He will actually provide CFO's to organizations that need that level of expertise, but can't afford to pay someone full time. It's almost like a "rent-a-CFO" concept. It's quite effective as the person who comes in with this level of experience can bring a wealth of knowledge to the table and the business he is consulting with gets a tremendous amount of value in the process. And you can take that concept with the CFO example and use it for Sales people, Marketing, Technology, etc. It's different than a temporary agency concept as it deals with higher-level professionals who bring true experience affecting a company's bottom line. A small business hungry for sales and professional management services would certainly find huge value in this type of individual.

Marketing is another area that many small businesses fall short. They may have a great product, great sales people and good finances, but they just don't know how to market the product. What they need help with is to create a comprehensive marketing strategy. Movie studios do a great job of this when they hype a movie. How many times do you see a movie trailer advertised and it's enough to get you to pay the $9 to go see the movie? They've created a significant "buzz" with the trailer to get you to go see the entire movie. It's the same thing with a small business. You, as business owner, or sole-proprietor have got to create a level of excitement or interest in your product or service, espousing how it provide all the things you promise it will do. I see this lot in the publishing industry. Without the hype and marketing around a new book, not many people would find the need or desire to buy it, correct? A good marketing executive will help a business find and identify this niche and appeal to that audience. Effective marketing for a small business is critical. Providing an "outsourcing" service for businesses to use a marketing professional service will be highly sought after by small businesses looking to grow.

If you decide to offer this service of "renting" professionals, sales people can also fall into this category. Like marketing professionals, sales people are often very costly and it may be less expensive for a small business to "outsource" this function rather than hire them as full-time employees. The outsourcing concept can also apply to other company assets such as office equipment, technology and shipping and logistics to name a few. You can look at just about anything a small business uses or consumes to run its business and find a way to offer that service in an outsourcing capacity. Businesses are interested in this concept because it helps them reduce costs and keeps inventory off their books eliminating heavy carrying costs.

If you have solid skills in training and education, helping small businesses with leadership skills development and succession planning are other areas you could consult with small business. Most small businesses don't spend enough time on either one. When a business is small, most owners don't really worry about leadership or the soft skills such as communication. Their main concern is getting business and satisfying orders, the day-to-day bread and butter of running a business. However, as the business grows and it begins to add people, the owner/operator needs to move his or her sights from manager/doer to leader. They can't continue to operate in their original arrangement, as they will not be in a position to help the business grow. They must develop leadership skills and learn to delegate the everyday operations to others in their charge. This must happen with every small business in order for it to make it to the next level. Providing leadership training and consulting is a much-needed service that a small business must engage. This is not only for the owner, but also for everyone responsible for leading a team of people in the business. If you have deep experience in the area of leadership training and like this type of entrepreneurial environment, you could find yourself in great demand.

Succession planning is another area where small businesses need assistance. As the owner/sole proprietor you've built a successful business, created a loyal customer base and provided jobs for many people. OK, once you're retired or you decide to pursue another venture, which person in your organization will take the reins once you're gone? Most small business owners don't really contemplate that reality. It's only a top priority at the point in which the owner decides to sell or get out of the business. Only then do they give it serious thought. Providing advisory and consulting services in this area for a business can bring to light the need for the business to do more forward planning on whom succeeds them in the leadership role. Big companies do this all the time. They start grooming leaders well in advance of the departure of the CEO. It is vital and necessary for a smooth transition as it can have a direct impact on the business and its operations. And besides, for publicly traded companies, Wall Street always has a keen eye on successors as it can have a negative impact on the stock price. The absence of good succession planning could be the difference between businesses moving forward seamlessly without its original owner or floundering in the dark while it struggles to find a successor.

I think its clear the business advisor and consultant will play a critical role as more business owners look for help to run their businesses more efficiently and look to improve the bottom line. Another niche of business owners comes to mind and that is minority owned business, particularly immigrants from other countries who may not fully understand the methods, techniques and requirements of running a business in the U.S. A good business advisor and coach can provide a wealth of knowledge to foreign-born business owners operating in the U.S. This market could provide an entire new source of revenue for your business consulting company.

I would say a good working knowledge of your geographic area and its potential marketing success of an incubation center would be a good place to start. The key here is to know the entrepreneurial climate and how many potential customers you might have that would use the service. The other consideration is the availability of office space. As I mentioned earlier, many cities overbuilt office space in the late 1990's and many are vacant. It would be a good idea to do your homework to find out where you can get a good leasing opportunity for office space at a reasonable price. One recommendation here is to find a good realtor that can help you navigate the commercial properties in your area. You might start with the realtor that sold you your home. Typically, they can handle commercial real estate listing and if not they can refer you to someone in their department that can help. It will be well worth your time to look carefully when selecting a piece of property so use as your incubation center. Also check with your local zoning commission to make sure you are within compliance of local zoning laws. There may be some considerations here as you look to operate a business in certain areas.

You're going to also need good interpersonal and communication skills. This is a small business opportunity that will require a lot of face to face contact with property owners, entrepreneurs looking to establish a presence for their business and other touch point with the public. You have to like and be comfortable within these situations and like being around people. A lot of your success will depend on your ability to market and sell your ideas to potential customers. If you have the right social and interpersonal skills, you'll be further ahead of your competition. Market your service wherever you get eh chance and opportunity. Remember, no one will be able to sell your services like you!

What are my start up requirements?

This business is definitely a business you can operate from home in a home office setting, however, you will definitely need to lease office space to set up your incubation center as we discussed earlier. Certainly, you'll need a good home/office PC to load some small business software such as Quicken to track your finances. You'll definitely want to start developing relationships with local real estate brokers to understand the market and where certain bargains might exist for office space. I would also begin establishing contact with different equipment vendors. Since your clients will be sharing equipment in the in a common environment, such and computers, printers, fax machines and phones; you'll want to find out where you purchase or lease this equipment inexpensively. You will recoup your costs by charging your customers a monthly fee to use the equipment and the space in the incubation center. You should also have relationships (if not already) with a good CPA who can help with the financial and tax ramifications of starting up this business. I believe strongly in this business opportunity and am confident it will grow over time as more baby boomers look to launch their own enterprise after their "traditional job" goes away.

I would start by visiting a local **SCORE** office which is part of the SBA (Small Business Administration) they offer advice to small business on many different topics and it's a great way to learn and understand what it would take to provide a similar level of service on your own. Many of the SCORE consultants are retired executives who enjoy working with small businesses within their particular field of expertise. I would also consider starting some small seminar (perhaps free in the beginning) at your local college and universities that center around specific small business interests (marketing, sales, hiring and succession planning) You can pick a subject that you experience and knowledge and offer the course to start-up entrepreneurs in your are. This is a great way to build credibility and to get a better understanding of what's required from your audience. You'll know pretty quickly once you start having the seminars what topics are important and which one's are not relevant to your audience. You can adjust and make changes as necessary once you better understand the need you are trying to fill. What you are trying to accomplish initially is to establish a presence in the market that you are an expert in this particular topic. You need to get noticed and have people begin to view you as someone who can help them and provide consulting services in a professional, valuable way. Once you've established this level of credibility it will open the door for other engagements.

Check out these additional resources to learn more about <u>small business ownership trends:</u>

Web Sites:

www.frbsf.org/publications

www.dmoz.org/Business/Small_Business/Associations/

www.sbaer.uca.edu/links/small_business_information/information.htm

www.varbusiness.com/sections/main/2005ii.jhtml

www.score.org/bp_4.html

Books:

Incubators: A Realists Guide to the World's New Business Accelerators, by Colin Barrow

The Ultimate Small Business Guide, by Basic books

The Small Business Start-up Guide, by Robert Sullivan

If you're Clueless about Starting Your Business, by Seth Godin

Best Businesses to Start Based on this Trend:

Owner/Operator Small Business Incubation Center

Small Business Consultant

Small Business Broker

Location/Developer for Small Business Incubation Center

Small Business Planner/Consultant/Advisor

Trend #3-Technology Innovation in Business

What's driving this trend?

This area, above many others, has garnered the majority of attention in the last twenty years. I remember, during my college days, professors discussing how technology and computers were going to enable businesses to do things quicker, faster and cheaper. It seemed like a dream back then in 1981, but needless to say the future did arrive and the world will never be the same. Technology has played a part in every aspect of our lives and will continue to do so well into the future. Now that we have a basic infrastructure in place, technologists will find ways to make things smaller, faster, cheaper and more nimble. Did you realize the computing power in the first hand-held calculator was greater than that used on the Apollo 13 missions! Think about that…It's astounding.

The world's first computer, the ENAC is now housed in a museum and takes about a full floor of space within the Museum of Natural History in Washington. Much has changed in the last 20 years, as technology companies have grown into large behemoths and creating millions and often billions for their founders. Microsoft now boasts a net worth greater than General Motors propelled by the move from a manufacturing economy to a service driven economy. In the 1980's we saw the introduction of the PC and client server computing and the move away from big mainframe computing. We saw an incredible explosion of software companies selling huge ERP systems to Fortune 500 companies that ultimately would run their HR, Financial and Manufacturing systems. These companies bought these systems faster than the software companies could burn the CD's. It was a time of incredible growth for the technology industry. The promise of huge savings, labor reductions and more efficient operations caused many companies to buy these systems to maintain their competitive advantage. It was a herd mentality. No one wanted to be left out when it came to having the best technology money could buy. Companies spent millions of dollars on the promise the software would help them run their businesses more efficiently. Some of it was accurate; however, many companies today have software sitting on their shelves that has never been implemented.

Then we ushered in the roaring 90's! This was the age of the Internet. We saw the same explosion of interest regarding leveraging the Internet as a viable business tool. Small, start-up companies raced to market to offer the latest and greatest dot.com business plans. The major flaw in many of these business plans was they didn't have a plan for long-term growth or a viable product that was matched with a specific need in the marketplace. They were also surviving on venture capital funds that flowed like an endless river during the boom times. However, the money did not last forever. Some of these small start-ups ran through millions and millions of dollars without earning a single dime in revenue! The company spent the money until the well ran dry. However, there is a bit of a silver lining, companies like eBay, Amazon, Google, SalesForce.com have bucked the trend and have shown revenue growth and built a loyal customer base. Both Google and SalesForce.com will make public offerings during 2004. These companies illustrate the fact that consumers will use the Internet to shop, do research and trade and auction items in a virtual marketplace. It also proves that many of these companies have the right business model and can sustain themselves on their own without relying on venture capital for an indefinite period of time. The one notable, irrefutable fact from the technology bubble is that technology is here to stay and will only accelerate it going forward. Technology companies will constantly strive for ways to increase speed, increase security and automate standard, routing functions.

As a simple example, think about pulling up to a fast-food drive-thru restaurant to order a meal. Typically, you speak into a speaker device as someone on the other takes your order. How many times are we bombarded with an offer to buy the latest "marketing package", "super-sized meal" ad blitz! You know what I'm talking about, right. How nice would it be to drive up to an automated keystroke system that allows you to key-in your order without ever having to speak to a crackling, annoying speaker system. Personally, I would welcome that level of technology. Everywhere you look routine functions are being replaced with automation. When you call your bank for status and updates to your accounts, you never speak to a real person. When I check on my investments, I get my information through an automated account balance selection. Wal-Mart, the largest retailer in the world is setting the trend with RFID technology (radio, frequency identification). Simply put, scanning devices will be embedded in the pallet and cases of product. When a truck arrives to deliver these products, automated information is sent through scanning devices to record shipment information, quantity, and inventory levels as well as stock out information when an item needs to be replaced on the retailer's shelf. What does all this mean-eliminating human intervention? If Wal-Mart can improve accuracy, reduce stock-personnel, loading personnel and administrative functions, it can simply save money and perform these functions automatically. Companies will embrace this technology, as the largest single expense is an employee. When you add up salaries, commissions, benefits and vacation the costs can be astronomical for any company trying to compete in the world economy.

Small-businesses that cater to the growing need of technology needs and that can leverage their capability and show value to a corporation will do well in the 21st century marketplace. After the technology bubble burst, companies both and small became very cynical regarding technology and the value it was supposed to bring to the bottom line. Many companies today still have millions of dollars of software on their shelves they never implemented because they overbought during the buying craze of the 1990's. So, a word of caution, if you intend to develop a business that is directly involved in the development of a new technology, you will want to do plenty of up-front research and marketing. You want to know beyond any doubt that your product has commercial appeal and will be able to save the company money or reduce overall cost. If your product or service can't pass those two tests, it may be time to go back to the drawing board.

I see other areas of technology emerging as well. These include *identity management; SPAM Control, Advanced Search Engines, Security, Satellite Radio and Biotechnology* to name a few. As mentioned earlier in the book, identity management will be a major area for businesses in the future. With the shocking terrorist attacks of September 11, 2001, the need for tighter security measures are needed more than ever. Companies everywhere who have major computer and hardware installations will be looking to protect themselves from hackers and electronic thieves looking to penetrate firewalls and gain access to company databases. Businesses that will do well will focus primarily in two areas-software aimed at thwarting hacker's efforts and software that helps to identify and authenticate users who are authorized to be in the system. I believe companies will benefit from hiring, "Professional Hackers" who are paid a fee to break into a computer system. Organizations will want to know where a hacker sees the holes or cracks within their security so they may effectively prevent future electronic crime. Professionals in these areas will do well in corporate as well as government environments. Corporations will also pay well for a comprehensive plan on how to avoid and prevent from being hacked. A well-developed plan on avoiding a hacking occurrence can pay off in dividends to a company looking to protect its corporate assets. Along this same theme, SPAM control software that protects children from seeing explicit material over the Internet will be another growth area in the future. Parents continually fret over protecting their children from viewing objectionable material. Companies such as AOL and others have implemented such strategies for current users of AOL; however, there is still room for other growing firms to provide a service and or product in this area.

Another area gaining momentum is advanced capabilities within on-line search engines. Most of the information written to date has been about Google which garners most of the press these days and seems to be the number one choice among users when looking to perform a search over the internet. Google boasts the greatest percentage of people using its tool to search from everything from golf courses around the world to detailed medical information to knitting groups in your community. It has become the de facto standard for searching on the Internet. However, it doesn't mean that Google will hold that perch forever. More highly sophisticated search engine capabilities are taking shape. Search Engines that can provide more detailed information regarding past use and history of the user. Other companies have developed the technology that allows for more narrow searches giving you highly specialized information based on your search request. My point here is to illustrate the fact that Google does not have a lock on this market. Yes, it was one of the first search engines of its kind and garnered a lot of press, however, other entrants into the search space will begin to pop up and provide competition for Google. My recommendation for this type of business venture is for someone who has spent a good amount of time in the technology sector, preferably with a search engine company. Learn as much as you can about this business and the technology and understand what the growing needs and trends will be going forward. I would also surround myself with high-quality technologists who know and understand the technology as well as the business side. Having one without the other is not beneficial. Understanding the business need is highly important in order to be successful in this business.

A customized search approach will begin to emerge as the next generation of search capability. Instead of a generic brand of search, new upstart companies will begin to offer queries tailored for an individual's tastes, interests, even location. These new companies that want to enter the search space want to extend the search into more realms and could be the next generation is search capability. Think for a moment the capability of having a universal search box on your desktop that lets you search archived email, local Word documents, and web pages with a single click. Many analysts and experts in the field deem personalized search as the industry's Holy Grail. The more information a search engine knows about you based on your whereabouts to your tastes in music, sports, or specific hobbies, the more it can tailor the results to your liking and delight you as a customer. This new search function will give birth to a "clustering" technology, which organizes results into folders. As an example a search on "skiing" might return folders under such headings as "hotels", "ski resorts" or "ski equipment".

These types of search capabilities might even be available as you walk into your favorite Wal-Mart store and giving you the capability of searching out sale items, new items or searching or a hard to get item. Over time, these search engines will devour every bit of personal information we want to divulge about ourselves, and it will serve up links that fit our tastes and locales-maybe even fine-tuning them according to the time of day. The market is certainly headed for dramatic growth and change.

In the 21st century marketplace, information is king! And search capabilities are the key to the kingdom!

There are a couple of other exciting emerging opportunities in the 21st century marketplace. These include Satellite radio and Biotechnology. Security is a huge area as we discussed earlier as organizations continue to look for ways to insure sensitive data is protected against potential viruses and computer hackers. Business opportunities in these areas will continue to grow in parallel with the threat of security breaches across computer systems, the Internet and other seemingly protected data repositories. Now let's move to a couple of other high potential areas. One of them has gotten a lot of press recently and that is Biotechnology. Analysts and others in the financial world claim the emerging technology and research being done by biotech firms will be the next wave of technology. This includes everything from gene-therapy, cloning, enhance medicines to DNA research. This field can prove fascinating! I read an article recently that talked in detail about scientists having the ability one day to test an embryo in a mother's womb to search for markers that would be indicators for cancer, heart disease and other catastrophic type illnesses that could be removed from the embryo before a child is born, eliminating the predilection of that child being born with the DNA roadmap for that disease. This is remarkable. The same could be true for Alzheimer's and other debilitating illnesses that have a huge impact on our medical care system and insurance claims in the U.S. The potential medical cost savings would be incredible. Other medical advances in the field would be to inject a capsule device into a patient that slowly secrets their needed medication in a timely way, eliminating the need to take pills orally and running the risk of forgetting to take the medication altogether. This has huge implications for the elderly who may not have someone to watch them on a daily basis to make sure the take the right level of medication and take it as prescribed. Another similar area would be to implant monitoring devices in people to gauge when a person would need to be treated for certain illnesses and to alert a medical professional (electronically) when a person would need to seek medical attention. The improvement in the quality of life would be enormous given these medical breakthroughs. As you can see from these examples, medical technology will have a huge impact on our standard of living and provide entrepreneurs with new and innovative ways to provide products and services into this marketplace. I would highly recommend this pursuit if you are someone who is trained in one of the specialty areas in the medical field to seriously consider looking into this market potential. You certainly don't have to concentrate on the areas I mentioned above, however, I believe the field of biotechnology and its intersection with human interaction will be an explosive growth area for the 21st century. I believe the human factor will also play an integral role going forward as well. The relationship between medical professional and patient will take on a more collaborative role versus the traditional position of a doctor speaks and the patient listens. Baby Boomer patients will take a much more active role in their overall health and life-planning and will look for non-traditional methods to help them maintain a healthy lifestyle beyond their retirement years. So, keep in mind, if this field looks like it might be of interest to you and you have the prerequisite medical background, please be sure you have the "soft-skills" as well. They will be as equally important.

You know, we've covered a lot up this point and I really am sincere when I say that I hope you are getting some really good ideas on what the future trends look like for the next several years and the brain is firing on all cylinders to help you determine what path you might want to take. The great hockey player, Wayne Gretsky was asked how he is able to maintain agility on the ice. His answer, "I skate to where I think the puck is going to be". Think about that statement. You might want to apply the same principles in deciding which avenue to pursue when looking at these future trends. If you can analyze where your skills and strengths lie and marry that to a particular business opportunity, the intersection of the opportunity and the trend is where the puck will be! I wanted to touch quickly on an area I will cover later in the book and that is to not quit your day job and to not give up if you truly believe in what you are doing. I say this because I've seen too many people quit a perfectly good job and spend their life-savings on a business idea, set up shop in an expensive office and spend a huge amount of money on advertising. Pretty much a "build it, they will come". They quickly find out that nobody comes! I firmly believe starting out small, keeping you full-time jobs and "testing" the market and your ideas one step at a time. By taking this approach you are minimizing your risk and learning as you go. Remember; just because you've started a venture on your own, does not automatically make you an expert. Treat this experience as a chance to go back to school, to learn, grow and develop as an entrepreneur. In all likelihood, no one taught you these skills when you were younger on how to run and operate a small business. Many of us, as I mentioned in an earlier chapter, never learned to be independent or to generate income for ourselves. So, give yourself some breathing room and learn from your mistakes. By minimizing your risks, you will allow yourself to learn and grow and not to feel too much pressure financially. I strongly support the belief that all of us have an entrepreneur in us and will have to develop these skills during our lifetime. All indicators point in this direction as companies downsize, offshore, lay-off and replace human efforts with automation. I believe each of us as working Americans owe it to ourselves to take responsibility for our destiny and learn the required skills to be more financially independent and to not rely on a corporation or government to support us during our retirement years. That, my loyal readers, should be our responsibility and ours alone.

I am excited to write this book as I have a deep, un-abiding faith in the human spirit and ingenuity. Throughout our history as a nation, we have shown the world and ourselves how self-sufficient we can be. I believe the innovation we exhibit can be found in individuals such as you and me. There is a huge transformation underfoot as Americans realize they have to take responsibility for their continued prosperity and leverage and harness their skills and experience and translate those into generating multiple streams of income. This is important for our generation, however, it will become infinitely more important for the generation coming behind us; our children. It will be extremely important for them to learn and understand the importance of self-reliance and to look and be sensitive to trends in the marketplace and dovetail those trends with business opportunities.

Since you are paying for the service, you can customize the stations you want access to and that may very well include a "Howard Stern" type show if that appeals to you. This reminds me a lot of what the early days of cable TV looked like in the late 1960's and early 1970's. I truly believe this same concept will take hold for radio as it did for television. Radio and television personalities have been pushing the boundaries of what's acceptable viewing for quite some time. I believe strongly that Satellite type programming will find a niche to cater to those who want to view alternative programming. As I mentioned earlier, for those of you interested in building or investing in this type of business, I believe there is a future here. If it does interest you, try and read up on as much information as possible on the subject. Try a Google search under Satellite Radio and I'm sure there will be hundreds of web sites on the subject.

And I'll end this segment with other golden opportunities that technology entrepreneurs will enjoy: Wireless Applications, Network Storage, Wireless Security, Grid Computing and Convergence Applications are the next hottest fields.

The 620 million cell phones and personal devices sold annually in the country are creating incredible demand for applications and content. Think camera phones and Blackberry's. Telecoms need new features to draw customers. Large firms like Microsoft also are buying apps and games for themselves or to sell through to users. Such applications can be cheap to develop--$50,000 can get a start up going and the market is expected to hit $15.6 billion by 2008.

Specialized storage networks are rapidly being replaced by cheap drives hooked up to the corporate network. However, this so-called network storage requires management software, and demand for it is expected to hit $7 billion in 2007. That means big opportunities for startups to sell niche products and features to major corporate computing suppliers like Dell, IBM, Oracle and others.

Wireless security is another rapidly developing area. The rush of advanced wireless communications technologies—Wi-Fi, Bluetooth, Wi-max, ultra-wideband—means that systems designed to secure and administer interconnected wireless networks are even more essential. The market is potentially huge; every major tech firm is a potential buyer-either to protect its own systems or to sell protection to its corporate clients.

Grid computing is the ability to cluster computers to sell processing power on demand, like utilities sell electricity, is slowly taking hold. There will be heavy demand for startups that create software to manage the clusters and for applications that capitalize on their massive firepower. Corporations will spend $12 billion on grid-computing technologies in 2007 by some estimates.

And one of the latest trends in technology is convergence applications. About 63 million Americans now have broadband, making high-speed home networks fertile ground for small startups. Online music, with expected sales of $1.7 billion in 2008, offers opportunities for applications that piggyback on Apple's iTunes and Microsoft's media Player. Video mail, instant message-based gaming, and the overall management of home networks also are areas where small start-ups can catch the eye of big companies.

After September 11, 2001, the need to secure a company's computer systems and our nation's borders has become paramount for our overall security as a nation. Companies today are spending an unprecedented amount on protecting their data and employees from cyber theft. They realize their reliance on technology has left them vulnerable to electronic breaches of security.

Security and identity management have become the number one concern for both businesses and individuals. Professional "hackers" who are able to breakdown and infiltrate a computers security and firewall are now hired by major companies to figure out how to protect them from future attacks. Worms, viruses and other computer "infections" are part of the daily news and media. No program, application or hardware is 100% protectable in today's complicated network of computer systems. Hackers and individuals make it their purpose in life to find ways to break down security and find a way in and steal precious information, bring down entire networks of systems and render business helpless in the process. The need for technically savvy individuals and consulting professionals have a huge opportunity to start out in this small, but growing market. Companies are very interested in understanding innovative ways to secure information and protect themselves from these types of attacks. The cost in lost productivity during the Melissa virus was somewhere in the 100's of millions of dollars. Businesses cannot afford not to invest in this type of security.

Unless you've been living a remote existence in some far stretch of the world, mostly everyone on the planet has experienced the phenomenal success of eBay. I believe when the thought of doing global commerce on the web was first thought of, eBay has to be the one company that fits that model the closest. It clearly is the free exchange and trade of goods and services at fair market value across the web. And it brings buyers and sellers together in a truly electronic marketplace. People who never sold a single thing in their life are now building whole businesses around selling their wares on eBay. The "Dummy" series books have sold thousands of books under that title, which clearly demonstrates the need for information on how to start up a business on eBay. Now, a word of caution, nothing is ever as easy as it seems. Of course, you're going to hear all the marketing hype about how easy it is and how much money you can make in a very short time frame- please don't be fooled and do your homework. Pick up the "Dummy" book I mentioned before and read up on as much as you can. Do your homework and truly understand the eBay consumer and what it is you are trying to sell and how marketable it really is. I don't think "following the pack" in terms of electronics, books and other common items already found on eBay will be the key to success. You could look at the opportunity a couple of ways. One is you could use eBay as a buying and selling medium to help you find items to resell through other means such as tag sales, garage sales, etc. Or you could find unique items yourself through rummage sales and the like and resell them on eBay. The key here though is to find one-of-a-kind items that set you apart from other sellers on eBay. Overall, I think eBay is a great selling and buying medium. It speaks to the future of how consumers look at buying products over the Internet, particularly for things they don't find in traditional retail circles. eBay has literally transformed the way people buy and sell products using technology.

If you think about the limitless possibilities, eBay has really established itself as the de facto standard on how buyers and sellers come together in an electronic forum. It has literally knocked down traditional boundaries for commerce and has given people the opportunity to buy and sell from anyone in world.

According to a July 2005 survey conducted by eBay, more than 724,000 Americans report that eBay is their primary or secondary source of income. In addition to these professional eBay sellers, another 1.5 million individuals say they supplement their income by selling on eBay.
Over 50,000 people in the UK draw a significant portion of their income from selling goods online. A study by the Center for Economics and Business Research (CEBR) shows that the average household boosts its earnings by GBP 3,000 through online trading.

Today you could buy watches, collectibles, cars, lawn furniture, etc. Tomorrow, you could be buying time-shares, pets, gasoline, a new home or an addition to your home. My point is it's unlimited what you could purchase with this on-line commerce tool. I would recommend that you try and find the "next generation" items that could possibly be sold over the Internet. If you try and start something similar to everyone else, your competition will be intense and you won't set yourself apart as a differentiator. Although, if you do decide to sell similar items as others, be sure you are giving excellent customer service, fair pricing, follow-up, free-shipping and making sure you follow up with a survey on how well your product and service were received. This will give you a solid reputation and will set you apart from your competitors.

The future in robotics looks bright. In the early years robots were mainly found on the manufacturing floor in corporate America, soon, however, robots will be found in America homes, doing everything from vacuuming floors to cutting the grass to dispensing medication. You were probably thinking that your exposure to robotics was going to be limited to the movies or science fiction quarterly, right? Well, think again! Robotic technology will play a significant role in the 21st century and it will make its way from the manufacturing floor to our homes, much the way computers and pc's did during the 1980's. Consumer use and adoption of robotic technology will be more readily acceptable as consumers find common and practical uses for these devices. As the technology becomes more user-friendly and the demand for its use begins to grow, the consumer demand will grow steadily during the next 10 years. One area I see growing is the robotic use by aging baby boomers. More and more retirees, due to better health and longevity will want to remain in their homes, as they get older. They will bristle at the fact of going to live in a retirement home and will want the personal freedom that comes with living out their many years in their own home. However, they may need help with this living arrangement. Some may need help with everyday chores within the household, such as cleaning and general house maintenance. Robots could play a huge role in this function.

From a recent article in USA Today, September 2004, robots could essentially fall into three categories: home bots, care bots and joy bots. Home Bots could be programmed to talk, remember speech patterns, and react to their owner's thoughts and concerns—they could even be trained to play cards or discuss current events.

What skills are required?

Probably the most significant skill required here is the innate ability to clearly see how technology can be adapted into a consumer's lifestyle or a practical business application. A good example of this is the company iRobot based in Boston. This company is regarded as a highly innovative company with its product called the Roomba, a robotic vacuum cleaner that can do everything a standard vacuum cleaner can do, with one exception; it doesn't need anyone to operate. It's totally self-sufficient and can clean a room independently, without any human assistant. I believe a company like iRobot in unique as it can "see the future" and create products that consumers don't even realize they need or want yet.

The greatest technology in the world will barely get noticed if there is not a practical usage for it in the market-place. If you are interested in getting into this area, you must have a strong desire to find out where the gaps are today with business and how technology fills a roll to plug the gaps. Microsoft comes to mind with their first release of Office. Before this release, there was not one standard of application that was in use for spreadsheets, word documents or presentations. With Excel, PowerPoint and Word, Microsoft brought these applications to the marketplace as a standard for all businesses to use. Soon, businesspeople across the U.S. were able to use a common approach to sharing information. Bill Gates had a vision of how technology could be applied to solve a common business problem.

What are my start up requirements?

I would say in this instance it would help to have a background in the technology market. It's helpful to understand what's occurring today and what the trends are when it comes to the latest adoption in technology both from a consumer and business standpoint. I would say get to know what's happening not only today, but what might be happening in the future. The greatest value you can provide is to get people excited about what the possibilities are they may not have even seen yet. Because technology changes so rapidly and is obsolete quickly, getting out in front of the latest trends will help to establish your credibility. Understanding what the technology of the future might be is only half the battle. Being able to show consumers or businesses how they can apply it to everyday problems and challenges is critical. Technology for the sake of technology will only go so far in its appeal. You have to show real value of how you can apply to solve real business problems. There are so many directions you can go in this field. If you have experience in software or IT consulting, there are so many possibilities that are open to you, particularly with small businesses. Remember, as small businesses begin to grow, their need for IT and the appropriate software to support their growing business is definitely something an IT consultant can become engaged. There's also the huge filed of software training and education. Consultants who are conversant in the latest business software and tools will have plenty of work in this field.

Small business, in order to look and act like their bigger counterparts will need help in the areas of enterprise software, wireless devices and mobile computing to name a few. If you have experience in this area, particularly from a bigger company, you experience will be in demand from the smaller companies. Leverage the experience you've gained for the last 20-30years and apply that to smaller companies who will pay quite well for your years of knowledge. Research, Research, Research! Set your sights high and leverage your years of experience in the technology field with smaller companies who value what you will have to offer.

Check out these additional resources to learn more about <u>business technology trends:</u>

<u>Web Sites:</u>

www.cutter.com/trends/advisory.html

www.eaijournal.com/PDF/EAITrendsRoch.pdf

www.marketresearch.com

www.daviniciinstitute.com

www.ebay-connection.com/

www.online-auctions-made-me-rich.com/

www.entrepreneur.com/ebaycenter/0,6316,,00.html

www.entrepreneur.com/article/0,4621,312476,00.html

<u>Books</u>

Trade Magazine "Business 2.0"

Trade Magazine Computer Age

"Emerging Memories": Technology and Trends, by Betty Prince

"Technology Trends" in Wireless Communications, by Ramjee Prasad

"Current issues and trends" in E-Government research, by Donald Norris

"Health Technology Trends", by Ecri

"New trends and technologies in Computer aided learning for computer aided design", by Achim Rettberg

"Electronic Commerce Technology Trends", by Weidong Kou and Yelena Yesha

The Video Production Organizer, by Alex Matza

Video Production Handbook, by Gerald Millerson

eBay business the Smart Way, by Joseph T. Sincliar

Starting an eBay Business for Dummies, by Marsha Collier

Secrets of eBay by Donny Lowy

Best Businesses to start based on this trend:

Retail -Hearing Aid store owner

IT Consultant to retail industry

IT networking and security consultant to small and medium businesses

IT Trainer

Wireless Communications Consultant

Video Production Business

Video Education and Training Business

Adjunct Professor for Video Production

Home-based business selling on eBay

eBay drop-off Center

Security and identity management consulting

Hardware/Software Reseller for Security Systems

Smart Home Security Systems

Education/Training Training for Corporate Security

Recycling of old and obsolete technologies (cell phones, computers)

Trend #4 – The Aging Population

What's driving this trend?

It will become clear in the next several years the magnitude seventy-six million baby boomer's retiring will have on the nation's economy.

They will affect everything from overall purchasing power, healthcare, travel, the social security system and the workforce to name a few. Their financial impact on the economic landscape will be felt for years to come. If you are looking for business opportunities, this area provides a wide view of how you can leverage this trend to start a business. All kinds of businesses will begin to sprout up, some that have already been in existence that will grow exponentially as well as new businesses that will be new and innovative to serve this market.

If you want opportunities that are poised to grow over the next 5-10 years, researching this market and their buying trends and lifestyle changes will certainly create an abundance of prospects. This segment of the population will be very different from the generation that preceded them. They are living longer, are much healthier and have a greater positive outlook on life after retirement. They will also have a greater level of disposable income, will be willing to travel and take vacations and spend a considerable amount on their grandchildren. They will purchase mobile homes, at-home services, adventure vacation packages (think of former President Bush skydiving for his 80th birthday coming up in May 2004!

They will also be purchasing financial services, exercise equipment, vitamins and health aids, cosmetic surgery and secondary vacation homes as well. And many will be self-employed as they take early retirement packages and look for ways to pursue a dream of being on their own. Many will find a way to be independent by utilizing their skills while they were employed and use those same skills in self-employment. The aging boomer population will care deeply about maintaining their health and physical appearance as well as their financial well-being. If you have skills in financial management, physical therapy, nursing and healthy-living consulting, you have an edge up on starting a business that coincides quite nicely with the boomer trends that will hit this country like a tidal wave! Many boomers will have made a good bit of money on their 401K plans or through inheritance and dutiful savings over the years. They certainly don't want to squander it and they want enough to live on and fund their lifestyle as well as leave some to their heirs. They will be in need of financial services businesses that can help them plan how to best leverage these investments over the next 25-30 years, since they will be retired many years after they stop working. If you are someone who is an accountant, banker or financial services professional, I would highly recommend you become certified in financial planning and look at this market as one that could drive huge potential revenue for you on the future. Participating in speaking engagements at local Rotary Clubs, Chamber of Commerce meetings and AARP meetings can certainly help to get the word out about your services and benefits you provide.

The exotic travel industry is an area that will experience significant growth as it follows the trend of the baby boomer retirement. Many boomers will have a significant amount of disposable income and will spend a portion on exotic vacation destinations. Many will want a custom-made vacation package that fits their specific needs. People who have a level of discretionary income at their disposal will have great satisfaction in planning a vacation that takes them through a ski vacation in a remote part of the world or a motorcycle trip through several countries in Europe. There are over 76 million baby boomers retiring beginning in 2006 and the market for these types of vacations will be huge. Many baby boomers will be receiving huge inheritance from their parents. This transfer of wealth is expected to be the largest intergenerational transfer of wealth in history. Many will use this new found wealth for relaxation and leisure activities.

Another area that will be of great interest to the boomer group is physical health and well-being. Remember the fitness craze that took off during the 1980's! The boomers in there 30s & 40s drove that trend. They realized the importance of good health and maintaining a healthy life-style early on in life. Well, guess what, they will want to continue that lifestyle as they get older. There is a web-site available called ediets.com that makes healthy-living and dieting very easy. You can virtually input your current physical information and it will compute BMI, target weight and several other target areas to concentrate on. And for a nominal fee it will create a diet and exercise plan customized to you as an individual. I illustrate this web site as an example to point out the validity of the trends that are becoming evident in society both now and in the future.

Pharmaceutical companies are spending billions of dollars on R&D to determine new ways of providing drugs to the growing baby boomer population. Many older Americans have high cholesterol, high blood pressure and don't necessarily have the right diet in place for their needs. Health-care consultants and professional who cater to this market segment on creating a balanced lifestyle and exercise program will do well in their own entrepreneurial ventures. Older Americans will certainly pay to gain knowledge about how they can improve their health and add more years to their life span.

A term you will most likely hear regarding the baby boomers is "aging in place". Although there will be an explosion in active adult and assisted-living facilities throughout the U.S., there are still many elderly people who want to grow old in the comfort and familiarity of their own homes. A recent study conducted for the AARP claims that a whopping 83% of homeowners surveyed said they would like to remain in their homes the rest of their lives. This market is certainly one you can start a business and or service around. For those of you inclined to be proficient at building and remodeling, you may want to consider offering remodeling services and doing small changes to an elder person's home such as adding extra lighting by the front door, or making larger adjustments such as raising the height of the dishwasher to make loading and unloading easier. You may even want to consider undergoing specialized training to understand the specific needs of the elderly, and learning how to make specific home modifications to suit those needs. In most instances, people don't have to spend a lot of money to make their homes safer. This will make it easier for people to justify the expenditure. Another service to offer before the actual remodeling effort may be a consulting service to analyze and determine based on a person's needs and the condition of their home what modifications might make sense. A free estimate or proposal might make sense up front, which can then easily turn into a paid event.

As you begin the proposal, look at the walkways to and from there entrance doors. As people age, movement becomes less precise so wider walking paths around the house are important. Be sure nothing is crowding the space where an elderly person walks to get to different points of the home. Eliminate tripping hazards such as cords, scatter rugs or thresholds. Stairways should be well lit and have banisters that extend to the bottom step. Also consider that elderly people lose their balance quicker than younger folks and should correct anything that is a struggle in their home, like sticky drawers and doors. Finally, elderly people should not climb up on anything.

For bigger type projects, experts say people in their 60's should start thinking toward making their home adaptable for later years-and any remodeling project done at that time should consider the future in case there's a need for a walker or a wheelchair. Other changes to consider are wider doorways with beveled thresholds to make access easier to reach, and bathroom vanities that have been adapted to provide easier access to sinks, especially for people with wheelchairs. Additional changes can include solid wood blocking to the inside of bathroom walls, in case there's ever a need for grab bars.

Please remember, you certainly don't have to be a builder or a large company that builds hundreds of homes per month. You can definitely start out as a small one-person shop offering basic remodeling and "aging in place" consulting to this growing demand among the aging baby boomers!

If I didn't already spend a few minutes on this topic, I feel strongly about this trend as well. And that is, the vast majority of older workers is currently employed and will most likely redefine the term "retirement". People will not retire the same way anymore. They will experience phased retirement, gradually working fewer and fewer hours. Some will not end full-time employment for years to come.

Current figures from the United States Bureau of Labor Statistics verify our assertion. Recent measurements of the American workforce reveal that of 4,864,000 people who are over 65 and willing and able to work, 4,657,000 (95.7 percent) of them are working today. Of this number, 2,550,000 people work full-time and 2,107,000 are working part-time (less than 35 hours a week). Breaking the statistics down even further, we learn that there are 2,705,000 people in the labor pool (working or seeking work) in the 65 to 69-age range, with 2,614,000 (96.6 percent) working. Of the workforce in the 70 to 74-age range, 1,156,000 of the 1,208,000 (95.6 percent) in the labor pool are employed. There are 888,000 in the 75 and over labor pool: An astonishing 472,000 (53.2 percent) currently work full-time and 416,000 (46.8 percent) work part-time. There are 319,000 in the 80+ age range workforce, with 309,000 (96.9 percent) of them working.

What you want to be able to do, as I've stressed throughout this book, is to observe the trends taking place and use your entrepreneurial insight to pick out how these trends translate to business opportunities. My intent in the book is to present these very real trends taking shape in the market and to help you map your skills and experience to an appropriate business venture. That truly is a winning formula for success! Think for a moment about this trend. How about a staffing service that specializes in placing older workers in suitable jobs? Or a transport service that helps bring older workers to and from work that may not be comfortable driving themselves because of their age. What about a resume service that helps older workers polish up their resumes for the jobs they may be applying. Many of these older workers may not have had a resume updated in 20 plus years. Someone who is a solid wordsmith can help create a brand new resume for someone who may not have the desire or ability to create it themselves. With your skill set, you have the ability to provide a much needed service!

What skills are required?

The aging of the baby boomers will provide hundreds of opportunities that require all kinds of skills and experience: technical skills, customer service skills, food service delivery and preparation, building and remodeling skills, interpersonal skills, and computer literacy skills, to name a few. 76 million people entering this next phase of their life will require all kinds of products and services. You'll need to do a clear assessment of your skills and strengths and then match those with the business requirements that are needed.

What are my start-up requirements?

Again, this will depend on what type of business you are going to start. Remember, most businesses that you start today can be managed from a home office. You will certainly want to consider this route due to the savings on leasing and rent that you would normally spend if you were to be in a traditional office setting. Another minimum requirement for any small business today is a good desktop computer package, preferably one with printer, fax, and scanning and copy capability. You may not think you need all this technology in the beginning, however, as your business grows you'll be glad you made the investment up front. You may also want to check into any time of training or certification you might need before you get start. Let's say for instance you wanted to capitalize on the vacation home-buying boom and wanted to be a home inspector. There might be specific requirements or training you might need to become certified. Remember also, certification in certain areas can separate you from your competition as someone who has put for the effort to become an expert in their field.

Check out these additional resources to learn more about <u>the aging population trends:</u>

<u>Web-Sites:</u>

www.secondfiftyeears.com

http://www.marketresearch.com/browse.asp?categoryid=945&g=1

http://money.cnn.com/2005/04/01/pf/expert/ask_expert/

http://www.bgassociates.com/marketing_to_boomers.htm

http://www.iqpc.com/cgi-bin/templates/singlecell.html?topic=236&event=9410

http://www.ml.com/index.asp?id=7695_7696_8149_46028_46503_46635

http://www.comingofage.com/

http://www.aginghipsters.com/blog/archives/cat_culture.html

<u>Books:</u>

"Is 50 the new 30? Have you considered how to reach…On Selling", by Bob Popyk

"Marketing to Leading Edge Baby Boomers, Perceptions, Principles, Practices, Predictions, by Brent Green

"Baby Boomers Turning to Retirement Planners", by Andrew Scott

"Advertising to Baby Boomers", by Chuck Nyren

"Prime Time: How Baby Boomers will Revolutionize Retirement and Transform America", by Marc Freedman

"The Baby Boomers Guide to Living Forever", by Terry Grossman

Start Your Own Specialty Travel & Tour Business, by Entrepreneur Press.

How to Start and Manage a Travel Agency Business: A Practical Way to Start your Own Business, by Jerre G. Lewis.

How to Start a Home-Based Travel Agency, by Tom Ogg

Best Businesses to start based on this trend:

Financial Planning Services

Nutraceutical Store

Estate Management and Trust Service

Boomer Zone Stores-(products geared specifically for boomers)

Robotics Distributor/Trainer (in-home assistant for boomers)

Smart Clothes Retail Shop

Eldercare Services

Custom Cremation Services

High-Tech Funeral services

On-line Specialty Travel Business

Corporate Retreat Specialty Travel Business

Audio Books/Books on tape

Hearing Aid Store (Retail or on-line)

Trend #5 –Employee Professional Training

What's driving this trend?

A large percentage of people entering retirement will seek information about starting a small business. Many of them will be coming from corporate jobs in which they have worked their entire careers. They will need information that will help them make informed decisions.

This will be a growth area for someone interested in leveraging 21st century marketplace trends. The need for education will transcend across multiple generations in the U.S. over the next twenty years. Public school students, in many instances, need supplemental education to help them with their overall educational needs. You may have seen such franchises such as Sylvan Learning Centers and Kumon Educational services in your area. These are franchise systems that are specifically dedicated to supplementing a student's overall public school education. Parent's today are willing to spend additional money to get their son's and daughters additional tutoring if it helps them on their SAT exams or their entry into their college of choice.

Another educational shift that is taking place is financial and entrepreneurial education for children. Public schools do not have a curriculum based around educating students on financial management or entrepreneurship. There really is no formal education process in place to educate children today in these areas. There is a growing need to fill this gap. Entrepreneurs who are willing to develop educational courses and schools dedicated to this goal will do well in this market. It's obvious today that we need this type of education as so many adults today carry huge credit card debt and don't have the fiscal discipline to manage their finances.

The other area that I think will experience significant growth is entrepreneurial education for children. Both children and parents understand today there is no security in working for someone else. The news headlines are filled with reports of companies downsizing workers who have dedicated themselves to the company and their work. Parents do not want to see their children go through the same level of uncertainty they themselves experienced during their working careers. A web-site called biz4kids.com is now available to children interested in starting a small business in their neighborhood such as lawn care, babysitting or general businesses that can be started up as well. The kits are available to children who are interested in pursuing a career in their own business. I had the pleasure of meeting with the person who started this small business and he is very committed to helping young people get a start in operating their own small business. I believe this will be a major trend with young people and they will need help and assistance and guidance as they try to forge their own path and not rely on a corporation to provide for their livelihood.

The third area I see as having high potential is adult continuing education. As adult workers, we constantly need to update and learn new skills. If you have training or skills on a specific area and one day you find yourself out of a job because it's been outsourced, you will quickly find out you have to regain new skills to compete effectively. This trend is happening all over the U.S. and in many industries, particularly technology. Workers today are faced with a huge task of retooling and relearning new skills in order to stay competitive in today's marketplace. The need fro training and educational courses will continue to increase as more workers are faced with this challenge.

Booming trends for computer repair are emerging and will continue to show promise as more and more small businesses are operated from home. There are several owner-operated businesses that are in operation today and several franchised opportunities in operation today. Many of these small business owners absolutely enjoy having a service that is available to them and can provide quick and expedient service at a reasonable price. Most owner-operated small businesses don't have the knowledge to fix and maintenance their PC systems at home so they will look to a business that can handle their needs. There are two ways to approach entering this space. You can build and develop the business on your own, or you can buy into a franchise operation. Both have their advantages and disadvantages. Building the business yourself allows you creative control over the marketing, products and services and financials. However, you might not be able to grow as quickly or have the backing of a name brand behind you that allows for quicker growth and expansion. A business like this, built on your own, will require a lot of marketing in the beginning, particularly if you don't have a storefront established.

A franchised business should have a clear and defined marketing plan established to help you get of the starting block very quickly. However, franchising this type of business may have upfront costs as well as royalty fees associated with it as well. A portion of your businesses proceeds may go towards royalty fees each month. These fees can be as high as 6%-8% monthly. And with a franchise type business, you will have less control over much of the decision making and may limit your creative abilities. I just think it's important to point out the pros and cons of each opportunity. What may be right for one person may not be right for someone else. I just think it's important for someone who is seriously interested to weigh all the possibilities and then make an informed decision. The marketing plan for this type of business is very similar in its approach as to the previous mentioned business profile. Again, I would highly recommend word of mouth advertising and speaking at the Chamber of Commerce meetings and the Rotary Club. Taking out an ad in your local business paper is not a bad idea either. And sending out flyers and our mailers to local small business owners can also prove to be a beneficial way to garner more business. The good news is that if you are good at this type of service business, word will get out and your reputation will speak for itself.

You can also set your clients up on a quarterly cycle of maintenance. This could mean automatically coming out once a quarter to replace toner in the printer, provide upgrades or fixes to their particular software and tune and make sure everything is operating in an orderly fashion. Provide the customer a 10% discount for future visits if they refer a new client. This will help to maintain a steady customer base and also help you get new business as well. Remember, friendly, reliable service is nothing to take for granted. If you provide those basic essentials with this business venture or any other business, you will be way ahead of your competition. I remember during one of the downturns in the economy and I was searching for work, a neighbor of mine started up a home-remodeling service, doing painting, sink replacement, laying tiles, you name it and he did it. When he told me what he was doing, I thought to myself, "Wow, how will he compete with the thousands of similar small-businesses doing the same thing he wanted to do". I didn't see how he would be able to complete. A few months went by and I saw him in the neighborhood and I asked him how it was going. He replied, "Dan, you wouldn't believe it, I've got so much business, I don't know what to do"! Needless to say I was amazed and happy for him. I asked him what his secret was. He said,"People are so excited when you say what you're going to do and you keep on that promise"! "That's all they really want"! It taught me a valuable lesson that day that so many small-business owners lose sight of the basic "blocking and tackling" of running a small business. Do a good job, finish it on time and charge a reasonable amount and customers will not be able to resist using your services. Forget the rule, and it will be an uphill battle.

I think we are just scratching the surface of the capabilities of what the web will enable people to do in the future. People are already consistently taking college classes, getting advanced degrees and leveraging the web to learn and become more knowledgeable. And there is room to grow in this space that will span across multiple generations. Both young and old alike will want to take advantage of the web and leverage its capability to learn about new subjects, get training or get a degree. If you are web savvy and have a teaching background, you probably have the right combination to develop a learning based web site to teach a wide range of topics and subjects. Think about how many colleges and universities are offering college courses and degrees over the web. The trend has exploded over the last several years and will continue to grow. Think about a pregnant mother linking to a web-site that would teach hear on how to nurse a baby through video instruction, showing her step by step what she needs to do well before her baby is born? And all this is done over the Internet and in the comfort of her own home. Or a dad or mom looking to fix a leaky sink or garbage disposal by getting on a web site called ufixit.com! And at this web site, there could be hundreds of links that show you how to fix hundreds of different repairs around your home. Think about what that homeowner would save in costly repairman bills or books he or she needed to buy to do the repair.

And it doesn't have to be limited to home repairs or feeding a baby. You could learn to play guitar, or understand how to start an import/export business through on-line web tutoring. The possibilities are endless! You could be the owner of ufixit.com! You think I'm joking right? But I am not. Remember, you are only limited by your own imagination and desire. If the mind can think it, it can be done. You don't even have to be the one who comes up with all the ideas or designs the web site or writes the content. If you can persuade others this is a good idea to start, then you can find the areas of expertise in others who share this passion for learning on the web. As you begin to create this group of talented individuals, you can share the creation of these learning web sites more easily. It's called divide and conquer and it will not seem so overwhelming. If you do decide to go down this path with a small business catering to e learning, it would be beneficial to determine the demand for such a site. Go and check out your local colleges and universities to determine what level of effort they are putting beyond remote learning efforts. Their response will help you estimate what level of interest is out there for this type of learning.

Other ways to gauge market demand could be to locate other web sites that are doing something similar. Hopefully, there aren't too many, which would give you the indication that you don't have that much competition. But if you are able to locate some, find out what they are offering? What is the quality? What kind of courses do they offer? How much do they cost? What is the quality of the web site? How long have they been around?
What kind of customer base do they have? You could pose as a potential customer and get a lot of good marketing information this way. The data you collect will be invaluable.
I find the best way for me to obtain and assess information if to find it myself. Ask the right questions. Talk to the right people. Ask probing

and in depth questions. Don't let people get off the hook too easily until you are satisfied with the answer you have received. If you are going to embark on this or any opportunity, those skills will serve you well.

Probably the most substantial information you might get is from friends and family. Casually mentioning these ideas in conversation can yield interesting results. It's funny in life how ideas you may have are things that people have been thinking about or would like to have, but didn't know how to get the product or service. All of a sudden, you mention something and they have an A-HA moment. Amazing! Seriously, don't underestimate how well-informed friends and family might be. You could really get some fantastic suggestions from sources you didn't even realize. Don't be shy about your ideas! Tell people! Don't forget, they could be your customers some day. Better to float ideas out there early, get the feedback and then refine your approach.

Once you have done your homework on the marketing side and you've determined a need for e learning in the marketplace, it's time to go to the next level and that is to determine what types of e learning courses will you offer? How will you build your web site? How do you market and promote your service? What would you charge for the service and for the courses? How do you manage the content on the site? Do you have financing lined up to invest in the site?

The key to success here will be networking. You will need to get out and talk to people, make presentations, do seminars and create a marketing buzz around your e learning business. The need is there, you will just need to cultivate it and listen to your customer's needs. I would also recommend getting some airtime on either television or radio. You might want to consider connecting with a local college or university to offer your courses. This would be a great way to align yourself with higher education and get your business offered through traditional college course offerings.

What skills are required?

It helps to have an educational background, but it is not absolutely a necessity. If you have a background in this field it helps to get a jumpstart in having the right skill set. If you are looking to create and develop the business and to hire others to do the instruction, then you will probably be ok. On the other hand, if you are more hands on and want to teach, then it might help to get some accreditation through a certified training course. Other skills required would be interpersonal, communication, and good solid marketing skills in order to sell and promote your services. You could have the best training and instruction courses available, but if no one knows about it, it's not going to get noticed.

What are my start up requirements?

Again, it depends on what type of training/educational service you plan to provide. Training can be delivered in many different mediums; instructor-led, web-based and even CD tutorials. I think the market for training and education will be huge in the next 5-10 years. Many out-of-work job seekers will need help getting re-trained in another field. Many people will abandon their original job choice and will look to learn new skills. Many people will seek information regarding entrepreneurship and how they can get started in their own business. The need for this type of training, I believe, will be huge! There will also be a market for young college graduates needing to better understand how to land that first job or how to prepare for that big interview. I think you can see the point here. There are literally hundreds of training opportunities out there depending on your area of knowledge and expertise. Keep this in mind, as the world gets more complicated and the need for specialization increases for job requirements, so will the need for training.

Check out these additional resources to learn more about employee professional training trends:

Web-sites:

www.humanresources.about.com

www.amanet.org

www.trainingmag.com

www.tregistry.com

Books:

Training for Impact: How to link Training to Business Needs and Measure the Results, by Dana Gaines

Running Training like a Business: Delivering Unmistakable Value, by David Van Adelsberg

"Absolute Beginner's guide to computer basics", by Michael Miller

"Computer Literacy basics", by Ann Ambrose

"Practical Computer literacy", by June Jamrich

"Computer Literacy and Careers" – CD

"Suggested Activities to motivate the teaching of computer literacy", by Joan G. Junger

Best Businesses to start based on this trend:

Corporate Training Services

Web-based on-line training courses

Career Counseling and Training Services

Computer training school for transitioned baby boomers

Computer training service to senior centers

IT Training Instructor at local college/high school

In-home training instructor for seniors

Small business consultant

IT Security consultant

Trend #6-Professional Home Services

What's' driving this trend?

Ask any busy professional couple and or parents and they will tell you the one thing they would like more of is TIME! Today's parents have less and less time due to demands from their jobs, children or their elderly parents. They simply don't have enough time in the day to run their households as efficiently as they'd like. Many things like grocery shopping, oil changes, pet visits, post office runs and shopping for a birthday present to name a few simply don't get done. There have been several concierge services that have popped up in recent years that cater to the growing demand for At Home Services. One business that comes to mind is one that's called, "At Your Service". This business appeals directly to the market for people who lack the time to do many of the necessary, but mundane tasks that need to be done. Typically, this type of business will have a menu of services they offer and you can pick and choose 'a la carte" style. Using only the services you feel is necessary to fit your lifestyle.

Starting up a business like this will require superior interpersonal skills, as you will be working directly with the public. You will need to develop a level of trust and rapports so people know you are dependable, they will likely use your services over and over again. You should enjoy these aspects of dealing with the public, as it will be more difficult to stay in business if you are not people-oriented. As you start a business like this, you will most likely be the one who is actually doing the errands until it reaches a point where you simply cannot keep up with demand. At that point, it will be necessary to hire some help. This is a good thing! First, it means your business is growing and secondly, it will allow you time to sell and market your business to other clients.

One way to market your services will probably be through word of mouth-Your existing clients will be your best form of advertising as they mention your services to their friends and acquaintances. Another sure-fire way to garner more business is through regular presentations at Rotary Clubs and Chamber of Commerce meetings in your community. What better way to have a captive audience to market your services?

This type of business will continue to grow, as people will constantly look for ways to carve out more time for personal time with family. If they could find a way to off-load some of the more mundane chores to a professional service, they certainly will. A few of the services that come to mind might include: grocery shopping, gift purchases, cleaners, bank deposits, post office and car repair and service to name a few. This type of business can also be translated to business type services as well.

Many small businesses that typically operate from home can use individuals who can run errands and take care of the many necessary business and administrative type activities. The same method for advertising for the personal shopping would work well for the business side. Chamber of Commerce, Rotary Clubs, etc. are all great locations where small business meets to learn about business services in their community.

What skills are required?

Skills required here would be a good sense of trend spotting and what is needed from your target market. It's important to understand what services will be needed as demographics and lifestyle changes take place in society. Whenever societal shifts take place among large groups of people, new and different needs will arise. There are several changes occurring right now. The first one is the lack of time among working professionals and the second one is the aging population among baby boomers. Both of these groups will certainly require professional services that help them make their lives easier, efficient and more productive. And they will pay for these services if they see the value they can bring to their lives.

There are many types of services that cater to busy professionals. Everything from landscaping and lawn services to retail outlets that let you buy a week's worth of homemade prepared meals. Being able to market your services with good solid interpersonal skills are extremely important. The important skill for this type of start up is to get your name and reputation established. Start out by creating a solid reputation and word of mouth advertising will begin to help you create more opportunity.

What are my start up requirements?

One of the key start-up requirements would be to research your competition. Who else is doing something similar? What services are they offering? How long have they been established? What do they charge for their services? My point here is to do your homework. The best way to get started and to insure a level of success is to do as much research as possible on your competition. You will be amazed at what you will find out and how you can offer new and different services your competition hasn't thought of.

Your advantage will be to offer services they haven't even thought of that they need! I would definitely recommend you start up in a spare room in the house to keep your expenses low. Create fliers and take out a small ad in your local newspaper to generate demand. Also, look into speaking engagements at your local Chamber of Commerce or local small business meetings to talk about your services. Many small cities and towns have monthly meetings where small business comes to talk about their products and services. You might be able to offer your services to small businesses as well as individuals. It all depends on how big you want to be!

__Check out these additional resources to learn more about professional home service trends:__

__Web-sites__

www.homehelpersfranchise.com

www.eldercarelimk.com

__Books:__

"The comfort of home: A complete guide for caregivers", by Maria M. Meyer

"Eldercare for Dummies", by Rachelle Zukerman

__Best businesses to start based on this trend__

In-home health care professional

Concierge Service for busy professionals

Professional Home Organizer

Handyman service business

Home Depot trainer

Home Decorator

Trend #7-Leisure Time Activities

__What's driving this trend?__

I'll touch on this topic many times throughout this book, as I strongly believe the baby boomer generation will be a mighty force as it transitions from the world of work to the world of retirement. They are the largest group of people in this demographic-76 million strong and their purchasing power will only continue to get stronger as they will have an incredible amount of disposable income to spend on leisure type activities.

Many of these boomers will try and recapture some or many of the activities they enjoyed as youths. I just finished reading an article that highlighted a boom in muscle car purchases. I'm talking about the classic muscle cars of the 1960's and 1970's-Barracuda's, GTO's, Camaro's and Firebirds. As Detroit continues to produce retro hemi's and newer versions of the originals, demand for the real thing will continue to have strength. And who do you think is buying these cars for $66,000 to$1.5 million! Yes, the baby boomers- men and women in their 50's and 60"s who remember these automobiles of their youth and an era that left an indelible mark on their psyche. They crave these cars that bring back memories of a simpler place in time. Now that they have the disposable income and the time to enjoy these activities, baby boomers will do what it takes to relive a part of their youth. Remember, this generation will not go quietly into their retirement years. They will go kicking and screaming while behind the wheel of a 450 hp 1966 classic Pontiac Firebird! Mark my words.

Classic Cars are not the only form of leisure activity boomers will seek. There are many other things they will crave to bring a sense of peace and harmony to their lives. Boomers will also seek out: *acting lessons, guitar lessons, knitting lessons, investment classes, real-estate classes, golf, sailing, and skydiving.* And the list could go on and on.... The point is that baby boomers will be in a perpetual learning mode and will seek to take advantage of their leisure time by learning and exploring new activities and hobbies. Baby Boomers will not be satisfied watching TV and rocking away on the front porch. They want to be active, they want to learn and they want to feel productive! This is definitely a trend that can be capitalized and leveraged through a business opportunity.

If you are proficient in any of the hobbies mentioned above, think about offering courses through the adult education program at your local high school or community college. If you are into extreme sports such as skydiving or white water rafting per se, you could be tapping into a whole market for seniors interested in these types of activities. Marketing and soliciting your business to this age group could bring huge results and not to mention the revenue stream. You may already be involved in these types of businesses and it just may be a simple point of directing your marketing efforts to this group of individuals.

One of my favorite leisure time activities is taking to the road on older-model GS450 Suzuki Motorcycle. Now granted, it's not as glamorous as a Harley, but it still provides that adrenaline rush of the wind whipping through your hair and the sweet smells of fresh cut grass and the sounds of nature engulfing your senses! Ah, I digress. Seriously, taking to the road on a motorcycle will be one activity you can be sure baby boomers will be engaging in great numbers. You can see the trend right now! Look at the success of Harley-Davidson over the past twenty years. They can't keep up with demand…Boomers in their 40's & 50's wanted to own one of these machines when they were 18 & 19 years old, but couldn't afford one. Now that they are established and have enough disposable income, they are running in droves to their nearest Harley dealer to recapture a piece of their youth. Harley riders across America engage in rides that take them to Daytona, FL, Sturgis, ND and other parts of the country.

The riders are typically lawyers, doctors, dentists and business people all there for the same reason. They come to enjoy the fellowship of other bikers. Harley has even patented the sound of their bike to preserve it's one of a kind sound! You can bet that boomers will enjoy this leisure activity for many years and Harley-Davidson will enjoy strong performance on the sale of its motorcycles for years to come. So, you're probably asking yourself, "Dan, how does that translate to a trend"? Well, let's think about that for a moment. First off, if you are so inclined, you can buy a Harley-Davidson dealership. That may be a bit grand, but then again, maybe not. Or how about an authorized web site that sell Harley-Davidson merchandise. Big portion of Harley's revenue now come form the clothing and accessories that bikers enjoy wearing on their cruises with friends.

And don't forget, you don't have to limit your product or service to Harley's. If you are a biker enthusiast, you can establish a web site that caters to older and vintage cycle and parts. Many boomers have or will purchase older bikes that need parts that may be hard to find through local dealerships. A web site set up specifically for these owners can generate a lot of interest and potentially a lot of revenue. If you are mechanically inclined, how about opening up a repair shop? You can offer your service in a generic sense and offer to repair all makes and models or you can specialize in certain makes and models: Triumphs, BSA's Indian's, etc.

Another suggestion might be to develop a publication and or newsletter that cater to motorcycle rides in different parts of the country. You can detail out routes, special places to see and the overall trip plan for biker enthusiasts who want to take a week or two of vacation on their motorcycle and travel through Alaska or Nova Scotia on their bikes. You can even translate this into a web site and generate ad revenue from advertisers to help support the site and provide a revenue stream for your business. You can then list ride packages across the country with pricing packages, other riders who are signed up as well as testimonials from rider who have made the trek before. They can provide a free form of advertising!

What skills are required?

The great part about leisure time activities for the baby boomers is that it offers many possibilities to leverage your skills and experience. If you like to write and you are creative you can develop a newsletter or web site specifically targeted for this generation that lists out activities for baby boomers in a particular geographic region. You can take the example earlier of the renewed interest in 1960's muscle cars and develop a web site that lists these cars for sale across the United States. Included in the web site can be information regarding shows, upcoming events and a section for buyers and sellers.

If you are good with people and know about computers, guitars, home repair, skydiving, travel, etc. you can build a small business providing instruction, information, and training on a many different subjects the boomers would have an interest in. The trick is to look at your skills, background and experience and determine what gets you the most excited! You will have great success if you follow a passion!

What are my start up requirements?

Your start up requirements will be determined by which direction you choose to go. It could be as simple as a spare room in your house with a computer, Internet connection and phone and fax line. Or it could be a storefront with a full inventory of products and services. My advice, however, would be to start off simple. Find something you truly enjoying doing and see if there is a need in the marketplace for this service or product. Test market the idea to friends, family and anyone who will listen. Get some good solid, positive, feedback, refine your approach and begin to target market your service through small ads, the Internet, or through speaking engagements. Find and take any and all opportunities to market and sell your product. Keep your budget small and keep focused on getting the word out about your offering.

Check out these additional resources to learn more about <u>leisure time activity trends:</u>

<u>Web-sites</u>:

http://findarticles.com/p/articles/mi_m3092/is_n23_v31/ai_13260546

http://www.marketresearch.com/map/prod/1466503.html

http://seniorliving.about.com/od/retirement/a/newboomerretire.htm

http://www.careercc.com/shopmall/html/mature_workers_package.shtml

http://www.fredericserriere.com/SeniorStrategic/liste_doss_cat.php?compteur=10&numcat=60&idrb=5

http://www.cafebabyboomers.com/retirement/Baby-Boomer-Generation-The-New-Retirement-Plan.php

<u>Books</u>:

Retire Retirement: Career Strategies for the Boomer Generation by Tamara Erickson

Prime Time: How Baby Boomers Will Revolutionize Retirement And Transform America by Marc Freedman

Retire Rich: The Baby Boomer's Guide to a Secure Future by Bambi Holzer

<u>Best businesses to start based on this trend:</u>

Exotic vacation adventure travel agency

Motorcycle tours through scenic and rural America (web-site or monthly publication)

Pilates and meditation classes

Classic car restoration classes

Computer literacy and training classes

Self-improvement classes

Guitar lessons/musical instruction

Golf Pro

Martial arts/self-defense Instructor

Trend #8 – Caring for "Mind, Body & Spirit"

What's driving this trend?

You've probably seen the marketing and advertising of many of these services over the last several years as more and more people are feeling the pressure and weight of raising children, working full time and managing the overall stresses of everyday life. At times it can seem overwhelming. And right now you might be asking yourself, how did my parents get through everyday without "massages", "aromatherapy", meditation and yoga? And to some extent that makes sense. But what I believe is that people today do have more stress in their lives and they are just as ill-equipped to manage it today as they were forty years ago. Death from heart disease and stroke are the leading causes of death in this country and stress related illnesses such as depression and anxiety have gotten a foothold in the U.S. today. We are a nation that has become over-worked and too dependent on anxiety and anti-depressant drugs. We must have the most expensive items, live in homes that are too costly, eat out more than we can afford and buy the latest designer clothes. And we pay for it all on credit! How could this not cause stress? We are constantly living outside or beyond our means and we refuse to live any other way. Americans today want the best and they have the credit card balances to show for it. Look at the rise in depression and anxiety disorders. More and more Americans take some form of medication for these illnesses and the sad part is our children our being affected as well. We put much of this pressure upon ourselves and continue to do so in the face of mounting debt and financial woes. Because of this, people are looking for ways to decompress and find ways to reduce their stress levels.

Nutraceuticals are frequently referred to as "dietary supplements" or "nutritional supplements" as in contrast to drugs that are active chemical substances used to treat an illness or symptoms of an illness.

Nutraceuticals currently represent a different approach to medicine, one based on nutrition and the health or wellness of the whole body. As such, nutraceuticals currently offer an alternative to certain types of drugs (particularly over-the-counter drugs); they have the potential to form a distinct market.

Consumers in the U.S. have an insatiable desire for nutrition based healthy alternative food choices. And manufacturers are eager to fill this need through introduction of new food and drink products that help consumers reach their individual health goals. With the population ageing and the increasing importance on health and longevity, this market is expected to grow to $25 billion in the U.S. by the year 2009. However, one the biggest obstacles facing manufacturers today is public distrust. Many don't' believe the claims made by the producers of these vitamin supplements. Newcomers to this business opportunity can take advantage of this distrust and turn it into positive results with positive marketing and fact-based studies. Present studies indicate that in Europe, young adults consume 36% more nutraceuticals and in the U.S. the figure is as high as 28%.

This trend does have its roots with the U.S.'s obsessions with good health. But I believe it will take on even greater significance as the baby boomers begin to age. They have always been a generation that embraced youthfulness and they will certainly endorse products that make them feel and look younger.

The market is huge beyond the baby boomers. Parents of young children looking for alternative healthy foods and snacks will comprise a huge market potential. Athletes looking for competitive advantage in their chosen sport can also be a large market for these energy and protein fortified foods and drinks. And you may think that nutracueticals are just for human consumption. Guess again. Avid pet owners are looking for healthy ways to get their pets to live to a ripe old age and they will spend the extra money in order to achieve this goal for their beloved pets.

What skills are required?

Many have found benefit through meditation, yoga and massage therapy. I truly see this as a growth area as the stress in our lives will not be going away anytime soon. There were approximately 24,000 certified massage therapists and body workers on 1999. That number will grow to 81,000 by 2004. This represents a 70% increase! You can pursue this opportunity through several ways. One is to offer courses through your local college or university on these different relaxation techniques. If you have your own massage therapy business, you can gain referrals through the courses you offer so you are establishing two forms of income streams. You can also have a retail shop that sells different aromatherapy oils, candles, books and other associated products that deal with relaxation and meditation. (Another area that fits in well with the relaxation trend is the drinking of tea as an alternative to coffee and also as a reducer of stress. It's key to remember the way this is marketed, as they all offer ways to reduce stress. The product or service is a means to an end). If you are a licensed massage therapist, you can offer your services as well. Already we've looked at several streams or forms of income with just one idea. It always amazes me how you can get creative on what you can offer in terms of product and services from just one idea. The secret is to think big and not to limit you when it comes to starting your business venture. Getting creative on how you can leverage one idea into several other income streams will give you a hedge against risk. In other words, if one area of your business falters, you at least have several other streams to keep you afloat. You don't have to stay within the yoga and meditation category either. There are other areas emerging within this trend as well. There are many retail stores that have been established that cater to people with back problems. These types of businesses sell chairs and furniture that contributes to relaxation for areas of the body that gets the most use have become popular in recent years.

What are my start up requirements?

I think having a strong background in massage therapy and relaxation techniques would be a good base for starting up this type of a business. It's important to understand, however, that knowing the specifics of being a good masseur doesn't necessarily mean you have the right skills to run a small business. The two aren't necessarily interchangeable. Being really good at giving massages and running a business requires separate and distinct talents. It would be to your benefit to take some basic business classes to understand how to write a business plan, marketing, sales and accounting. If you are new to this type of business, try and get involved in the business through working in a reputable establishment to learn and understand how such a business operates. It will be an incredible learning experience on how these businesses market themselves and make money. You will be able to learn what works and what doesn't and be able to take that information and apply to your own business.

Check out these additional resources to learn more about <u>mind, body and spirit trends</u>:

Web-sites:

http://www.all-natural.com/art-indx.html

http://www.mbspirit.net/

http://www.lifeorganizers.com/spirit-mind/

http://www.wellness.com/

http://www.bodymindspiritjourneys.com/

Books:

Yoga, Mind, Body & Spirit: A return to wholeness, by Donna Farhi

The Atlas of Mind, Body and Spirit by Paul Hougham

Body, Mind & Spirit: Daily Meditations

Body, Mind, Spirit: Tapping the healing Power within you, by Richard P. Johnson

Achieving the Body, Mind, Spirit Connection, by Brian Luke Seaward

Best businesses to start based on this trend:

On-line wellness and vitamin store (brick & mortar or web-based)

Pilates and fitness class instructor

Herbal tea and desert shop

Relaxation class instructor

Corporate instructor on healthy living and lifestyle changes

Physical Fitness Instructor for busy professionals

Personal Trainer

Trend #9 – Improving Financial Literacy in the U.S.

What's driving this trend?

The plain and simple fact is that baby boomers remain woefully ill prepared for their financial future. They are not prepared to live another 25-30 years without a steady stream of income. This fact, quite honestly, will create a tremendous market for financial planners and professionals who want to offer services in this marketplace. My people have invested a lifetime into their work and you expect upon your retirement to enjoy the fruits of your labor. Unfortunately, many people don't realize how ill equipped they are for retirements until it's too late. They don't know how much to save, how to build an investment portfolio or know much about retirement tax law so they can enjoy 10, 20 or 30 years of retirement security. Many people will retire, but will be forced to go back to work full time or part time in order to maintain a certain lifestyle. Because of years of poor planning, they will not be able to afford to quit work altogether.

There are approximately 77 million baby boomers born between 1946 and 1962 and they are slowly making their way toward retirement. Based on these statistics, some are 10 years away or less if you look at age 62 as being the "unofficial" age to retire. They don't know how much to save and to appropriately invest in order to create a portfolio that will last a lifetime of retirement. Only 25% of Boomers are confident about their investments and feel on track for a comfortable retirement. The remaining 75% are going to wake up too late to do anything about their dilemma. They will most likely have to keep working past the usual retirement ages of 65 to 70. They will have to look at working either part time or full time. Boomers shouldn't count on Social Security benefits. No one knows whether Social Security will still be around, or at what age you'll be able to claim benefits. The government could raise the benefits age by five years or more to preserve the program. From a financial perspective, I see a generation that's on the verge of a crisis. Furthermore, only 20% of the Baby Boom generation has a company retirement plan (and even less than that take advantage of it). The other 80% are on their own.

Further studies indicate that most baby boomers were never properly instructed about saving money. They weren't taught this during their school years. Keep in mind, their parents lived through the depression and as a result money was a foreign subject in many households. Then we had the glorious days of the stock market boom of the 80's and 90's which gave the false impression the stock market could bail you out. Everyone knows how that turned out. It created an illusion that if you invest in the stock market your money will continually go up in value. In today's economy, you have to know how to think about money, especially long-term investments that yield income. Most boomers don't understand this concept.

Many of the common myths are that boomers are well-prepared and savvy about money or they will receive a huge inheritance from their parents. I think if you were a boomer today and planning on a comfortable retirement, I wouldn't count on or assume anything. The good news for folks like you, who are interested in developing a second source of income or small business career, is that boomers can use all the help they can get in the coming years. Developing a business that caters to boomers and their financial needs will, in my opinion, be a success. This generation will not go quietly into retirement and they will want to enjoy the finer things in life and they will need good, fiscal discipline to afford these luxuries in life.

A small business that can help them with saving for retirement and how to build the best portfolio for long-term income as well as getting them the most from current tax laws will certainly do well catering to this market. They will also need assistance in planning for healthcare needs (Medicare) tax planning and shelters, retirement homes, individual stock tips and picks and don't forget 401K and IRA options, insurance issues as well as vacation tips and other lifestyle features. Their biggest challenge will be learning how to retire comfortably. This involves learning how to allocate their money, when to allocate it and into which type of investments. Boomers will need to be educated on how to maximize their savings, create the most return for their money and to get it to last through out their entire retirement. The focus of any small business venture targeting this market should concentrate on investment planning, employee benefit planning, insurance, estate planning and tax planning. Your typical "customer" could be anyone over the age of 45, thought even younger folks may want to get a head start. However, if you are 55 or older, the pressure is on. You're at the leading edge of the baby boom generation and you have a limited time to earn money and sock it away.

The business services you offer can take the form of consulting services, estate and tax planning as well as financial planning. A good way to market is to try teaching or writing an article for publication explaining the benefits of upfront planning and how it can provide value to baby boomers. This validates your ability and gets you recognition at the same time. You can then capitalize on this and offer courses at your local college or high school.

What skills are required?

A strong financial planning background is a good place to start. If you currently work in this field you have a leg up due to the fact you understand this business and you already have some ready-made clients. Strong people skills and a desire to help are also very important. Similar to the small business advisor, this is a customer-facing role and requires strong interpersonal skills. Your customers will need to feel a level of confidence and respect for you, as they will trust you with their financial future. Developing these types of relationships takes time and doesn't happen overnight. You want to build some successes and references early on to show potential customers what you're capable of in this business. It's much easier to get new clients if you can show demonstrable results. New clients are more apt to use your services if they can hear about you from others.

I think strong marketing skills are another key skill requirement. I know I've mentioned this quite a bit in this book, but I can't overemphasize it enough. Knowing how to market effectively and gain new business is the key to success in this type of business. After all, it's about selling yourself, your capabilities and your value. I can't stress this enough! I would also suggest a strong desire and appreciation for planning. This is an important skill requirement. Most people you will interact with won't have a strong inclination to planning and fiscal discipline. Most people today don't have the patience to plan effectively to meet their lifetime goals. They will be looking to you to help them in this area. You should really like to plan, organize and execute a strategy in this role.

A solid understanding of financial planning, investing and life-planning goals are very important. If you don't have a background in financial planning, it would probably help to become certified as a CFP or ChFP. There are web sites available that help you navigate how to become certified in these disciplines. It will make sense to become certified if you do decide to pursue this small business opportunity as it gives you more credibility if your customers know you took the time and effort to become a certified financial planner. If you know of someone who has already gone through the process, pick their brain for a while and get a better understanding of how they achieved their goal.

If you think you have what it takes regarding the right skill set and the right temperament, I believe this area has huge potential for folks interested in helping the boomers manage their financial futures. The boomers will have a huge level of discretionary income in the trillions and will be the recipients of the largest inheritance in history. My point is there is a lot of money out there that needs good, capable management. Start doing your homework and get a piece of this growing trend!

What are my start up requirements?

Your start up requirements in this area should be focused on getting an education about this type of work and what it takes to be successful. The more research and homework you do upfront, the better chance you have of being successful. Talk to as many people as possible that are already doing something similar. See if they like it. Ask questions. Spend a day with them, if possible, to see what a typical day looks like. The education you will receive will be incredible! Put a business and marketing plan together to help determine your goals and strategy. Putting it on paper will better help you navigate how you can reach your goals. Do some research on similar type businesses in your areas? Who's doing it already? Call them up and pretend to be a client and ask probing questions about what they do, and what services they offer. You will be amazed at how much you will learn from this exercise. You also be able to determine quickly what services they offer and how you might be able to offer better overall service. Many successful businesses become even more successful then there rivals because they are able to study them and offer better service. Don't be shy about calling and comparing to see how you can be creative and offer a superior service or price!

Check out these additional resources to learn more about financial literacy trends:

Web-sites:

http://www.ecponline.org

http://www.mymoney.gov/

http://www.jumpstart.org/

http://www.cde.ca.gov

http://www.frbatlanta.org

http://www.basic-skills.co.uk

Books:

Personal Financial Literacy by Joan Ryan

Financial Literacy for Teens

The Secrets of Money: A Guide for Everyone on Practical Financial Literacy by Braun Mincher

Saving and Investing: Financial Knowledge and Financial Literacy that Everyone Needs and Deserves to Have! By Michael Fischer

Improving the Financial Literacy and Practices of Youths: An article from: Children & Schools by Sondra G Beverly and Emily K Burkhalter

Best businesses to start based on this trend:

Financial Management class instructor (colleges, high schools)

Certified Financial Advisor

Publisher/Writer for financial publications

Speaker/Author (subject matter expert on financial independence)

Small business advisor on finance/planning & investment strategies

Trend #10-Changing U.S. Demographics

What's driving this trend?

During the turn of the century and at the end of World War II, America saw a changing demographic landscape. Millions of immigrants, leaving their homeland with nothing but the shirts on their backs came pouring into the U.S. for a better life. These immigrants knew intuitively that a better life awaited them across the Atlantic. Many of us were too young to remember the tall ships sailing into New York Harbor bringing thousands of people from Europe into the warm embrace of the Statue of Liberty. The dream of starting a business for many people in other countries is still very much alive today. The U.S. is still a symbol of hope, opportunity and a chance at a better life for millions of people throughout the world.

New groups of immigrants will continue to migrate to the U.S. over the next 10-20 years as people of Mexican, Indian and Asian decent continue to populate the country. This is nothing new as we have seen this demographic change already taking place. Immigrants from many countries know how to embrace the American Dream. They know instinctively that hard work; perseverance and the right attitude will allow them to reach their goals in this great country. Many start their own businesses and go to school to do whatever they can to leverage their abilities and maximize their potential. They understand intuitively the advantages hard work brings. They also understand the value of education and that sending their children to college brings more opportunities for the next generation. This approach was no different than when I grew up in the Northeast.

Many second generation Americans, my parents included, visualized the same American Dream of working hard and taking advantage of all this country had to offer. My small town in Connecticut was filled with second generation Americans of Jewish, Italian and Polish descent. They all wanted the same thing for themselves and their children. They wanted a chance to do better than their parents and for their children to achieve the American Dream. The next wave of immigration will want the same opportunities. So, if you're looking for a trend or an opportunity, much like the aging baby boomers, this trend will certainly open conditions for sharp-minded people to take advantage. The possibilities are endless in my humble opinion.

The immigration trends among, Hispanics, Asian and Indian descent potentially represents a huge marketing opportunity to cater to their needs, wants and desires. One of the first needs for these groups could be an education on American business and finance. Many of these folks will want to start a small business and will need an education on American business ethics, laws, and accounting and start-up information. Providing a service such as this would be invaluable as they may have little to no understanding of what is required to launch a business in the U.S. Helping them to formulate a business plan and marketing plan would be a major step in insuring they have the right tools to be successful. The more they can understand the more value you bring to them and their business.

You could start marketing your services through the Department of Immigration as a start and offer seminars and small business consulting courses, specifically geared toward this market.

Another area I think will need to be filled is entertainment services, particularly restaurants and other offerings that are native to one's homeland. People who migrate to this country will be lonely and a bit homesick for familiarity of their homeland. Identifying these areas of how you can satisfy their desire from their birthplace will certainly do well. And if you do it right, you may be the only place to procure or get such services and products. This would all depend on your location and proximity to the population you are trying to serve. The services and products you offer can vary from food, clothing, grocery products bookstores and the like. It's important when looking into this type of business to try and determine what products they can't get anywhere else but at your location. That will be your marketing hook!

Other areas for people migrating to this country could be speech and language courses. In order to be successful in the U.S. they will have to know and understand the English language. If immigrants cannot master the written and spoken language, it will put them at a severe disadvantage, particularly from a business perspective. Courses geared toward these two subject areas will do extremely well if you have that kind of passion to teach. You can accomplish these in many ways through local community colleges, on-line courses and adult education courses at the local high school. I would include in this series of courses on one financial planning as well. People from other countries would do well to learn our financial systems and how to invest their money for a solid return. Courses that offer the basics of investing can help foreigners learn what it takes to invest their money, how to save and to learn about the stock market in the process.

I think another area of importance to this market will be a placement agency specifically geared toward the immigrant market. I don't believe anything like that truly exists today. It could be the forerunner in its category. The reason I think it would work is that you are catering to a specific market that could potentially have specific skills companies or businesses are looking for in a candidate. And with the American workforce shrinking because of the aging population, cultivating an immigrant workforce could provide able workers to a lessening U.S. workforce. The placement agency could also provide job training, communication skills as well as the language and speech skills I mentioned earlier. Many companies typically need to be in line with EEOC (Equal Employment Opportunity Commission) and would find your service very valuable in order to meet Federal regulations when filling certain job requests. I like the sound of this business opportunity as it could a first of its kind. It's definitely worth looking into if you already have many of the skills required and has worked in the placement and temporary business before.

One of the areas most evident in the rise of the Hispanic market is Univision: the nation's largest Spanish-language media titan. There are some 37 million Spanish speakers in the U.S. that account for 13% of the nation's population and spend roughly $520 billion a year. Their numbers are expected to grow about 15% y 2013. By then, the amount they'll spend on cars, refrigerators, stereos and even soda could exceed $1 trillion. New companies emerging to cater to this group would do wise by trying to reach them through Univision. Hispanics are watching more Spanish-language television than ever before. Ten years ago, this group split their television time 60-40, watching more English television than Spanish, according to Nielsen Media Research. Today those numbers are nearly reversed and Univision commands an 80% share of the audience.

So, what this confirms is the growing trend toward an increase in population in the Hispanic demographic. This ethnic market will need all types of services going forward.

I also think areas like newspapers and newsletters catering to this niche group of immigrants can also prove to be a good business venture. People from other parts of the world are always interested in what's going on in their homeland country. Newspapers dedicated to that specific news and written in their language would certainly be welcome by people looking to connect with their roots. The demand for this type of publication would be strong, as you would have a captive audience drawn to the newspaper in an effort for them to connect to their countrymen.

What skills are required?

I think a key skill here is to truly understand this ethnic market. It might be beneficial to segment which market you'd like to study and try and focus within that area and become an expert. To stay current, you'll need to read as much as possible on the demographic changes and needs within the market segment. You might find newspapers or magazines dedicated to the particular ethnic population to research what are their current and future needs. You may also want to spend a good amount of time on the Internet researching web sites that cater to your demographic. Web sites dedicated to these growing markets will increase as more and more people join on-line communities to stay connected. Familiarize yourself with these sites and make a point to go out and surf information that can help you determine current needs. Look for emerging trends and see if you can determine if this is something that has potential for a small business or enterprise. Spotting trends is often a key component to starting a small business. Seeing a trend before anyone else sees it gives you a huge advantage.

You may also want to spend time with your target group observing current products and services that are being offered to this specific demographic. Recent statistics in August 2005 show large increases from 2000 to 2004 in the Hispanic population across many metro counties in the U.S. For example, in the year 2000, Parmer, TX, had 49% of its population as Hispanic and in 2004, it is now 55%. The same was true for Murray, Ga. It had a 6% Hispanic population in 2000 and 12% in 2004. It's clear how the numbers are growing and will continue to grow in the future.

What are my start up requirements?

A good solid thirst for information and statistics is a good start up requirement. You have to be hungry for information and want to do the research in order to determine what this target demographic needs in terms of products and services. You might also want to consider doing focus study groups and take samplings of this population to help you better understand how this target group buys their products and services. What do they look for in a product? Price, Place, Promotion, Product (the 4 P's of marketing) always plays a role in how you market, regardless of the demographic. Creating a survey and asking probing questions about their buying patterns and history will help dramatically in your research on how you market to certain demographic populations.

Check out these additional resources to learn more about the changing U.S. demographic trends:

Web-sites:

http://usinfo.state.gov/journals/itsv/0699/ijse/capop.htm

http://www.alliance2k.org/asian/PowerPoint/2001/sld013.htm

http://www.centerforpubliceducation.org/site/c.kjJXJ5MPIwE/b.3633965/

Books:

How we're changing: demographic state of the nation (SuDoc C 3.186:P-23/) by U.S Census Bureau

Changing demographics cause shift in market share (SuDoc C 3.205/8:91-20) by U.S Census Bureau

The changing U.S. population and the future labor force.: An article from: Business Perspectives by Clifford C. Clogg (Digital - Jul 28, 2005)

The U.S. Budget & Economic Outlook 2006-2015 by U.S. Congressional Budget Office

The changing workforce demographic issues facing the federal government: report to congressional committees (SuDoc GA 1.13: GGD-92-38) by U.S. General Accounting Office

Best businesses to start based on this trend:

Grocery/Food-Stores catering to specific ethnic tastes/demographics

Instructor on business ethics/entrepreneurism/finances to emerging demographic population

Publications – (newspapers, magazines, newsletters) that cater to emerging demographic trends

Language translation services

Daycare services

Eldercare services

Financial services

Ethnic restaurant (depending on region and ethnic population)

Trend #11- Career Counseling & Career Coaching

What's driving this trend?

By now you are probably getting the message that I really think the baby boomers (76 million) of them will create many of the vast opportunities for entrepreneurs over the next 10-15 years. There are 76 million of them heading toward retirement or for some a change in career direction doing something they truly enjoy. My prediction for this group pf Americans is they are a restless bunch. They are significantly changing the meaning of "retirement" and will redefine its meaning completely in the coming years. For one thing, they are a restless group. Remember, this group was born between 1946-1962 and lived during the most peaceful era of American history and most had the benefit of a college education. Boomers expectations, skills, experience, earning potential and disposable income are much greater than generations past. Their minds are wired differently as well. They will simply not be happy with the status quo; they want more and will expect more. This is typified with the increasing divorce rate among this category. Boomers set the tone by pushing up divorce rate levels to 50% or greater. There view on marriage is that it too is disposable. If you're marriage is not working out and it becomes too difficult to maintain, life's just too short to waste time on something that is not going to work in the long term. This, in essence, is a boomer's attitude toward what makes them happy. They will not stay with something just becomes it's the right thing to do or that because marriage is a bedrock institution. If they are not happy, they will not continue to live under stressful conditions. Remember, in their minds, life is to be lived and not meant to live and suffer in silence as past generations.

And this holds true in their professional lives as well. Many boomers are not satisfied with their current work and careers. Many are dreamers and have a hidden desire to do something totally unrelated to their chosen profession. Many boomers will seriously evaluate to determine what truly makes them happy. I happened to be watching

Georgia Public television the other night and caught a program on a local business-man here in Marietta that services vintage motorcycles like the one's we road when we were kids in the 1970's. It was fascinating for me for two reasons. One, because I love the motorcycles he was refurbishing as I road them myself as a teenager, but the other reason was that here was a boomer (my age-44) who was deeply involved in a business that he truly loved doing. It wasn't even like work for him. This was something that was a passion and a joy and not like work. I was amazed and thrilled at the prospect of someone who was that enthralled with what they did for a living.

I've got a good friend who lives in Tampa, FL who loves working with people and runs his own placement firm for finance professionals. He says it is something he absolutely loves doing. Boomers in the future will seek out this type of work. Work they love. Or better yet, work that feels like play. They will want to blur the lines between the two. No separation. Boomers will want it all-too have the ability to do something they always dreamed about doing, but couldn't do because of financial obligations.

I think this trend opens up tremendous opportunity for people already in career services or human resources or even human psychology. Career counseling will be huge for this population segment not only for individuals looking to pursue a passion in their own business, but for those who want to change career direction completely. Statistics point out that many people given the choice would change their careers and pursue another course of work if they could. Many new workers to the workforce will probably change careers *seven to eight times* during their working life. But boomers will certainly engage these types of services. They will want to consult with a professional who understands what it is they are trying to accomplish and then helping them put a plan together to achieve those goals. I look at this service as life and career planning goals and boomers will pay for this handsomely. You see, money is important to the boomers, but fulfilling their inner needs and giving them fulfillment in their life's work is more important. To be equipped to offer this service to boomers, having a background in human resources or personal development and or career development would be a plus. A background in business and teaching as well as psychology would also be advantageous. You will need to enjoy people and like helping to shape their future. This type of work can be very rewarding and can be extremely satisfying as you will have a direct impact on helping to shape a person's future direction and course in life.

Marketing your services and yourself will be the key to success. And there are many ways to do this in order to build your reputation and credibility. Speaking engagement at trade shows, HR conventions and small business gatherings are a good way to seek out potential clients. Another avenue could be Franchise seminars offered in your town or community. I attended several here in the Atlanta area and the audience is perfectly suited for people looking to change or shift careers. The very reason they are attending a seminar like that is to change direction. A perfect fit, right? Local Chamber of Commerce meetings, Rotary Club meetings and SBA (Small Business Administration) gatherings can also be a good source for clients. Be prepared with a good introduction as to what your service offers and how people can gain value and respond to your seminars or individual coaching sessions. Make sure your introductory presentation is brief, but enough to get them curious about what you can help them with. The more interest you can generate initially, the better off you will be in gaining momentum. Remember, you don't get a second chance to make a first impression.

What skills are required?

The baby boomers will not go quietly into retirement! They will redefine the way they will spend their "golden years". Many will not want to retire in the traditional way their parents did. They will desire to stay active and productive and many companies will recognize their worth and will find ways to retain them as creative members of the workforce. Understanding this demographic will be an important skill to acquire if you would like to pursue this as a small business opportunity. You have to really understand the wants and desires of these baby boomers and what it is they want to accomplish in their later years. What will make them feel fulfilled? What pursuits do they want to be involved in? Do they want to further their education? Do they want to start a small business? Do they want to pursue a life long hobby? Do they want to travel? These are just a few of the many questions boomers will ask themselves as they begin to examine how they will spend their days after a certain point in their lives.

A key ingredient to this business pursuit will be your desire to help people plan out their future. Do you like to plan and strategize? Do you like developing interpersonal relationships with people and enjoy communicating ideas and listening to others? These are certainly the most important qualities you'll need when deciding if this is the right opportunity for you. You might want to use yourself as an example. Once you've sketched out a preliminary business plan and you have an idea of how you would conduct a planning session, try it our on yourself first. You would ultimately be the best judge to determine if it flows and works for you. You'd rather work out the challenges with yourself first before you engage with a potential client and you find out it doesn't work.

What are my start up requirements?

Do your homework, first and foremost! Study the baby boomers and gain a greater understanding of what they will be looking for as they begin to enter their retirement years. Spend time with them; conduct workshops, surveys and seminars to help educate you on their needs. The information you gather from these sessions will be invaluable. The information you obtain will provide the basis toward how you will conduct your counseling sessions. You may also want to consider developing a series of worksheets that have different categories such has family, career, and hobbies that help your clients walk through what's important to them within these major categories. Each of your clients will have certain things that are important to them and it will help to see them on a worksheet so they can rank them in order of importance and how they see these areas affected after they retire.

I would also spend some time on several web sites that cater to this growing market. Sites such as retirementoptions.com have non-financial services they offer that have to do more with life-planning services after retirement. There is a lot of good information out there that can help you decide what counseling services are the best one's for you to offer.

Check out these additional resources to learn more about career counseling trends:

Web-sites:

http://www.careerplanner.com/

http://www.careercounseling.com/

http://careerplanning.about.com/od/careerchoicechan/Career_Choice_or_Change.htm

http://www.usnews.com/articles/business/best-careers/2007/12/19/best-careers-for-a-changing-job-landscape.html

http://www.careercc.com/after40.shtml

http://www.nytimes.com/2007/05/01/business/smallbusiness/01webcareers.html?ex=1335758400&en=6a254a8b3f39d6bc&ei=5124&partner=permalink&exprod=permalink

Books:

Career Counseling: A Holistic Approach by Vernon G. Zunker

Career Information, Career Counseling, and Career Development (9th Edition) by Duane Brown

Introduction to Career Counseling for the 21st Century by Robert L. Gibson and Marianne Mitchell

Career Guidance and Counseling Through the Lifespan: Systematic Approaches (6th Edition) by Edwin L. Herr, Stanley H. Cramer, and Spencer G. Niles

Best businesses to start based on this trend:

Career counselor for college students

Career counselor for senior level managers considering a career change

Image consultant

Small business advisor on talent management/HR/succession planning

Web-site planning service for career changers/college students

Trend #12-The Growing Demand for "Customized Products and Services"

What's driving this trend?

During the beginning of the industrial revolution, manufacturing companies prided themselves on uniformity and mass-producing products in order to keep their costs low and their products cheaper. They also provided a homogeneous product to the market without much differentiation to customers. Think of Henry Ford's comment for the Model T-"a customer can have any color they want as long as it is black". That kind of fit the relationship between a seller and buyer of goods in the early days of the 1900's. My, how times have changed. Nowadays, you can get any type of color, size, shape and customized product or service you want. The pendulum has swung in the opposite direction. Companies and businesses are bending over background to provide customers with customized versions of products and services that used to be available in only several versions.

The trend occurring on the market today is to help people identify with products and services as their "own". And what I mean by this is that consumers today want to feel as though they have a relationship with the company and the company understands their individual needs as a consumer. People don't want to feel as though they are treated like everyone else. They want to feel they are being catered to as specific consumer with individual tastes, needs, desires and wants. Businesses or your business specifically will do well to find out how you can appeal to your customers and consumers that make them feel as though you understand your specific needs and wants. It will require research and determination on your part, as you will need to get inside the "mind" of your consumer base. The key here is to focus not so much on an individual person, but a group of people with similar tastes and desires. This is your way of targeting a niche type of audience with specific marketing techniques toward this segment. An example might be the "tween" market of girls and boys ages 12-16 years old. And within this market you have concluded through your market research that teenage girls really like nail polish that is different in color and texture to many of the standard brands that are available today. They may like colors that match their mood or hair color for example. If you are able to design this type of product that ties into teenage girls personal preferences, then you have successfully "customized" your response to a specific need.

Or maybe along those same lines you can design a game-boy game for the "tween" boy segment that appeals to their sense of individuality. Any way you look at it, personalized products and services are gaining momentum and will gain in popularity as people move away from buying mass-merchandised products and look for items they can claim as their own.

One of the most prolific examples of this trend is the move from "mass media" to "personal media". No other example in my mind crystallizes this more so than Apple Computer with the iPod and Shuffle. Apple has literally created a revolution with these technology wonders. Consumers have the incredible ability to reshape the way they listen to music. They no longer have to pay for a pre-formed music CD for songs they don't like or care to listen to. With the advantage of Apple's products, a listener can create his or her own personal music experience. It is completely customized to a consumer's own tastes.

If you are able to come up with ideas that "fit" with this trend, you stand to make millions of dollars on your idea and invention. The key here is to find a product or service that blends the need for personalization with a growing market phenomenon. And it's not just about technology or music. I've read stories about sportsmen who dream up a perfect form-fitting chair for fishing or camping. The chair completely fits the needs of outdoorsman and those who purchase the item feel as though it was constructed specifically for them. From a marketing stance, they truly believe the manufacturer had them mind when they built that particular chair. Makes sense, doesn't it?

What skills are required?

A thirst for knowledge and information! Customization and personalization of products and services is certainly a trend that will continue, however, you have to understand what areas to focus on. Some products may not be conducive to customization. Doing the proper research upfront on which products make the most sense for personalization will help you define your niche and which market you'll need to go after. There could be many products that could be customized; however, picking the right one's can mean the difference between success and failure. And you don't have to limit yourself to existing products. There could be many opportunities to develop new customized products that haven't even hit the market yet. As companies continue to focus more on specific consumer needs, the growth in specialized products will persist.

Market research will be a key skill requirement if you want to find out what products make the most sense for customization. There is a web site called trendwatching.com that focuses on how trends like customization translate into new products. Spend some time taking a look on the web site and you'll be surprised about how much you'll find out!

What are my start up requirements?

Once you've had a chance to develop your market research, you probably want to spend some time assembling it on a spreadsheet to review your data. You may want to categorize your information into different buckets that show how these products might satisfy different needs by product category, demographics and income level. Once you've done this you can begin to segregate which ones make the most sense.

You'll quickly find which items make the most sense after you compile your list.

Check out these additional resources to learn more about customized products and services trends:

Web-sites:

http://tools.cisco.com/dlls/tln/page/research/detail/rs/2006/2020foresight

http://www.sciencemag.org/products/globaltext.dtl

http://findarticles.com/p/articles/mi_m0DTI/is_n8_v24/ai_18517692

http://www.wikiscm.com/wiki/index.php/Mega-trends_In_The_Globalized_Supply_Chain

Books:

Phrases That Sell: The Ultimate Phrase Finder to Help You Promote Your Products, Services, and Ideas by Edward W. Werz and Sally Germain

Growing Modular: Mass Customization of Complex Products, Services and Software by Milan Kratochvíl and Charles Carson

Customized your World. (Wireless technology): An article from: CMA Management by Andrew Tausz

Markets of One: Creating Customer-Unique Value through Mass Customization by James H. Gilmore and B. Joseph Pine

Service Oriented Enterprises by Setrag Khoshafian

Mass Customization: The New Frontier in Business Competition by B. Joseph Pine

Best businesses to start based on this trend:

Product or service business that caters to individual needs

Personal Trainer

Web developer for on-line time capsules

Personal Jewelry designer

Customized Gift Baskets for People

Customized Gift baskets for pets

Personalized funeral services

Designer clothing based on computer generated images

Trend#13 -The Growing Business Need for "Information Workers"

What's driving this trend?

I've always struggled with the term "knowledge worker". What exactly does it mean? Who are knowledge workers? How do you make, sell and distribute knowledge? Many leading economists continue to state the U.S. economy is moving away from a manufacturing based economy to a service based economy. For the past twenty years, U.S. manufacturers have been moving jobs to China, Singapore and other locations in the Far East where labor is much cheaper. The bottom line is labor costs in America have become too high and have made us non-competitive in many industries. The manufacturing sector has known this for quite some time and now professional positions, mainly IT professionals are the next group of workers to find their jobs being outsourced. It is a trend that will continue as U.S. companies continue to compete in the global market.

So, the one big message I take away form all this is that we (the U.S.) is moving away from "making things" to managing the flow of information and knowledge. Confused? Well, me, too. Well, think of it this way. Many of you use the Internet for personal use, and work, etc. Well, think about all the information you are sending about yourself when you make a purchase, let's say, on Amazon. One purchase on Amazon can tell someone about your buying patterns, how often you buy and other information about your demographic situation such as age, income bracket, marital status, etc. What do you think Amazon or other companies do with this information? You guessed it! They use it to sell you more stuff. Or they sell it to other marketing companies that in turn sell it to other companies interested in selling to you! Confused? You shouldn't be. What I just described is at the core of the information revolution. You see, with technology so pervasive in today's society, businesses, governments, and the educational systems to name a few can gather and process information at the speed of light. Information is everywhere! It's almost too much. Sometimes we feel we are inundated with all this information, we don't know what to do with it all.

Another example is making information more available to consumers and also to potential consumers. For instance, upon completion of this book, I will be looking to get it published, marketed and sold while trying to keep my expenses as low as possible. I believe I am able to do that through the information I've gathered regarding on-line publishers. Information and technology are now available to enable to be a first time publisher and get my work edited, published, marketed and sold through one avenue. This is the main reason the Internet holds so much promise and possibility. It is information rich and has the potential to transform the way we do business, search information, and buy products from cameras to airplanes. My point is that we are becoming an information rich society. Information is everywhere. However, the key is to term information into money or hard dollars.

I know your next question is going to be, "well how do I do this"? And how do I benefit from the information revolution? One of the terms you've probably heard recently is "Infopreneur". It's a term that became know in the mid-1990's and continues to gain traction as we move into the 21 century. The basic notion of the term denotes a person or persons who are able to make money buy selling information. Take for example a small company that wants to learn more about its customer's buying patterns and spending habits. An Infopreneur would be the person directly responsible for researching the information through the Internet and marketing studies, packaging it up to the client and selling it for a profit. I believe the infopreneur will become more prominent in years to come, as companies both big and small will want to cull through the vast amount of data and information and utilize it to reach customers in innovative ways. Companies may not want to staff these roles internally and may farm them out to independent contractors. This is where you can make a significant impact. If you have a strong desire and interest to research and find out information from various sources you could be a very good fit for this type of work. It will require skills that enjoy digging into to information and making sense out of good data versus the fluff. You will then need to know how to package and sell it to your prospective customers. Companies today are trying to manage the best way to spend there marketing dollars and how to best reach current and new customers. The best way for them to truly do that is to be armed with the most current and updated information on their customer's buying habits, spending patterns, and demographic information. If they are going to spend their marketing dollars wisely, they have to know where to target the dollars in order to give them the highest rate of return.

Another interesting area I have found in the area of knowledge and information is experiential marketing. You may have heard this term several times, particularly in regards to Nike town. Nike town was a classic example of Nike's willingness to immerse their customer's into the Nike Brand experience. It is a way to reach customers outside traditional marketing techniques. Volkswagen and Heineken Beer have done similar marketing programs and you can become a "Volkswagen" for a day or a bottle of beer for a day. These marketing experiences are designed to give people a total view of the product and a particular brand. It allows customers to become engaged with the experience of designing, marketing and the selling of a product. It allows a consumer to become part of the branding experience, rather than just being bombarded with images and media overload.

The experiential marketing is another type of the move toward an information-based society. Consumers want to be reached by companies in innovative ways. They are tired and bored of traditional marketing themes and want to be excited in how they interact with the companies they buy from.

Another key area that will continue to flourish in this new millennium is the buying and selling of information. Information is king! I mentioned this earlier. This was very much in focus during June of 2004 when an AOL employee was jailed for selling 92 million names to a source who then sold it to spammers who then emailed these unsuspecting AOL customers with advertisements from everything from kitty litter to timeshares. The main message here is the premium for this information and the price companies are willing to pay to understand consumer's buying patterns and demographic information.

My suggestion here is to find a way to (legally) sell information to companies that allows them to expand their marketing and sales reach beyond their core audience. Another form of information selling is to sell information based on trends and future statistics on demographics and buying patterns. Companies are constantly looking at their changing customer base. If you had the ability to supply this information to organizations before the change occurred, you would be in good stead and your skills would be highly sought after. An example might be a recruiting agency that is trying to determine possible clients in their geographic region that could benefit from their services. They may be trying to increase their database of potential job seekers and may employ someone like you as n independent contractor to research the demographics in that area. You could assemble a database of information of which people might be looking or currently out of work, age group and salary requirements. You could also break this down by specific industry category such has: healthcare, manufacturing, financial services and human resources. A good source for your information gathering could be the department of Labor, Networking groups as well as church associations. Once you've compiled a comprehensive list, you could sell it to many or all firms interested in the information.

Another way to solicit your services is to a new business just starting out in your area. Perhaps, there is a day care center or new restaurant that wants to open, but they don't know the demographics in that are. For instance, the daycare may want to know the number of stay-at-home moms and the number of children that might be potential customers. The fledging restaurant may want to know what the eating preferences or tastes may in that region, as well as salary ranges. This information would be extremely helpful to the restaurant management as it may determine type of food, price range and menu selection.

I have a neighbor in Atlanta that does something very similar for Wal-Mart. He pretty much goes out on "scouting" missions to determine the best locations, demographics, property assessments and proximity to high growth areas. The information to Wal-Mart is invaluable to the folks responsible for deciding where to build their next store. He operates his business from his home so his overall expenses are minimal. Peter had a good start as he worked for the company prior to striking out on his own. I would highly recommend this approach if you can do it. If you were able to work for a company first and establish yourself and your credibility, it would reduce your risk factor considerably. Remember, making initial contacts, establishing a reliable work pattern and understanding the industry or market you are working in at the expense of another company is a great combination. If you can start off in that direction, you will be that much more ahead of the game.

What skills are required?

You should have a love for doing and research and uncovering information! If you have a passion for digging through information and discovering facts and poring over figures, then this could be a good opportunity to follow. Becoming an independent knowledge requires patience and perseverance. The amount of information available on the Internet is overwhelming. It will be important to have good organizational skills to navigate through the vast amount of data that exists in cyberspace. You will need to have a good command of technology and how to find your way around different search engines and to use a computer to find and search out information.

You will also need superior skills on how to gather information quickly and to able to synthesize the data so that it makes sense to someone who may or may not have particular knowledge about that subject. Just because you may be good at researching data, you must also have the ability to interpret it and how you can transform it into valuable information. For instance, if you are working on a particular project and you've uncovered a lot of facts, figures and statistics, how can those numbers be turned into information for you client that can help drive more sales, provide competitive information or help reduce costs in their organization?

The key to research and analysis is the interpretation of the data and how the recipient can use it effectively. Doesn't that make sense? If you think you've got the right skill set to be a knowledge worker in this 21st century economy, I don't think there will be a shortage of work any time soon. If you do work for a small, medium or large firm, they all need help gathering information and understanding how the data can help them improve their business.

What are my start up requirements?

Don't hesitate to invest in a good, powerful computer that has enough processing power to handle your search requirements. And make sure you have high-speed Internet access as well. The last thing you want to deal with is dial-up service, when you are trying to meet a deadline for a huge customer project. Make sure you put together a good solid marketing plan. Your number one key to success will be your ability to get your name and reputation established in this market. You'll also want to establish a solid marketing plan. Your key to success will be to communicate who you are and what you do. The way to get started in this business is to design a solid marketing plan that allows you to communicate to potential customers your services and your value. Always remember in your marketing efforts to position "what's in it for them" or WIFM. Your customers are going to want to understand what they get from your services and how you can increase the value of their business. That is what will get their attention.

Check out these additional resources to learn more about information worker trends:

Web-sites:

http://en.wikipedia.org/wiki/Knowledge_worker

http://www.microsoft.com/enable/aging/infoworker.aspx

http://www.csiro.au/science/ps7c.html

http://ideas.repec.org/p/cvs/starer/96-41.html

http://portal.acm.org/citation.cfm?id=1089107.1089134&coll=GUIDE&dl=GUIDE&CFID=71981000&CFTOKEN=59430158

Books:

Knowledge Workers in the Information Society (Critical Media Studies) by Vincent Mosco

The supply of information technology workers in the United States by Peter Freeman

The Emerging Markets for Librarians and Information Workers (Library and Information Research Report, 56) by Nick Moore

REPORT WRITING: GUIDELINES FOR INFORMATION WORKERS by PAT F. BOOTH

Best businesses to start based on this trend:

Surveyor/Analyst for retail industry

Market research analyst for large companies

Market Research Analyst for small entrepreneurial companies

Independent information broker

Independent research analyst for government agencies

Virtual Assistant (Virtual Administrative Services from your home office)

Boomer Web-Site offering Special Discounts (to seniors) from various retailers

Trend #14 -Pet Ownership

What's driving this trend?

I never thought I would see the day when people would start a business and get paid for watching others people's pets! It's simply remarkable. But hey, we live in a society that puts a high premium on convenience and time. People today will pay what it takes to give them more time and convenience. My son has actually watched the neighbors' pets while they were away and was paid handsomely for it. With many families in which both parents work, and with children's after school activities and a rather hectic lifestyle, people today feel less in control of their free time, if they have any free time at all. Working parents today are tired and look for ways to get more flexibility in their lives. This tend coincides with the increased surge in dog and pet ownership. People today are just buying and owning more pets that ever before. A recent study in *"USA Today* stated that in 2006, $38.5 billion was spent on pets with the corresponding breakdown: food-$14.5 billion, medicine-$9.3 billion; veterinary care-$9.2 billion; grooming and boarding-$2.7 billion and live animal purchases-$1.9 billion. Very impressive numbers when you consider entering into a business that focuses on pets and pet ownership.

I am very confident that if you love animals and people, maybe not in that order, you can start a small business in this area very easily. I live in a very suburban area in Atlanta and the amount of dog owners is probably every other house in the cul-de-sac. What do people do with these pets when they go to work or go on vacation? You guessed it! They typically hire someone to watch their pets. These pets have to be fed, walked and exercised during the owner's absence. Its piece of mind the owner gets when he or she knows their pet is being well taken care of during the day.

It's always interesting to me how a business like this can start out as basic dog-sitting, but can turn into other services offered as well. You could offer home-delivery services for top-quality dog food. Or you can offer a shuttle service for owner's who need to get their dog to the veterinarian or for a shampoo and haircut. You see how once you've established yourself in one area; you can begin to branch out into other services. And marketing for your services can be quite inexpensive, particularly if you rely on word-of mouth. Once you begin to build your experience and reputation, other pet-owners will begin to want your services after they see and hear about it from your references. It will be a ripple affect as you leverage the free marketing from your existing customer base.

Another area that could evolve as you expand your business is breeding dogs. It would be a natural extension of what you are doing already. I am always amazed at the cost of some pure-bred puppies, particularly Labradors and Golden Retrievers to name a few. Some of these puppies can fetch as high as $300 per puppy! That's a serious return on your money. If you breed a dog that is highly sought after, (concentrate on breeds that are good around children) as most people who buy a puppy have children. Most parents would be skeptical about buying a Doberman puppy due to the reputation. So, if you do decide to go into this type of business make sure you are breeding the right type of dogs that people will want and love.

If I were to start this business tomorrow, I would probably do the following: Put fliers out in your neighborhood, post fliers at your local strip malls and advertise at place like Petco and other retail outlets for pets. I would also advertise at veterinarian's offices as well.

Well, let me digress for a moment. I just got back from vacation in the Northeast and to be honest I love the feeling you get upon your return from a well-rested vacation. You feel rejuvenated, rested and refreshed. I especially needed the respite particularly as I write this book. It was encouraging taking off two weeks and traveling to my boyhood home in Hamden, Ct. I saw the spirit of business ownership even in my hometown. Many small business owners were capitalizing on the changing demographics in the Northeast of the aging population. I saw many landscaping services and healthcare companies catering to this new niche! It was very exciting to see this as it lends credibility to the fact that as our population ages, older folks will need help doing things they once did before, but may be too physically demanding. The aging baby boomers, as we've discussed will be happy to pay for these services as it frees them up for other enjoyable activities. I guess I was compelled to detract from my message because of the energy I felt while I was on vacation…Now granted, walking on the sandy beaches of Cape Cod was reason enough to feel a sense of renewed energy, but the main reason was the people I met and talked to about their desire to be independent and to find a calling to start their own business. Many of the people I spoke to I discovered that starting their own business gave them a sense of independence and made them feel they were in charge of their own destiny. Many of them were disillusioned by working for others and wanted their "freedom" to make their own decisions.

The experience and conversations I encountered during the break renewed my faith in the American Entrepreneur and made me realize that most of us have the ability to break free from traditional thought processes of how we earn a living.

Another area that ties into this business service is specialty treats and foods for dogs and cats. I get called constantly from organic pet food services that want to sign me on as a customer and deliver organic dog food to my door. Their value proposition is that their food is better and has more nutritional value for your pet. You also get the convenience of having your pet food delivered directly to your door. You may think to yourself this is service might be a fad, but more and more people are signing up for this service because they want to provide the best care and food for their pet and they like the convenience of pet delivery.

What skills are required?

Well, first and foremost, a love for pets! You really have to be an animal lover. Not just a little bit, but a lot. Your passion and enthusiasm for animals will show through to potential customers and they will come to trust and respect you to care for their pets. Building trust among your customers will be your best marketing tool as you begin to solicit clients. If you've already been doing some pet-sitting for friends and neighbors, you've already got a head start on building your reputation. You will be surprised as people begin to mention your name to others and before you know you are getting referral business! And to be honest, once you've established a loyal base of customers, word of mouth advertising is the best form of advertising as it is unsolicited and it's inexpensive!

If you are going to pursue this business opportunity, I would also make sure you have some basic skills training in managing animals. Taking a course at an obedience school will certainly help to show customers you have the right credentials to care for their pets.

It will be important to have superior interpersonal and communication skills when working with your customers. The main thing they will be looking for is trust. If they feel as though they can trust you, then you've won them over. If they have the slightest doubt they can trust you with their pet, then you are not approaching the situation in the best manner possible. Remember, earning their trust is the key to success.

What are my start up requirements?

Getting out there and doing it! Do some pet sitting for friends, or your neighbors. Get some experience and see if you really enjoy it. The best way to get involved is to jump right in! You will accomplish several things by doing this: 1) you will actually see if you like it. 2) You will have minimal risk as you will be in trial mode and not really busy so that you can assess your interest. 3) You will receive feedback from your neighbors and friends on how well you did.

Check out these additional resources to learn more about pet ownership trends:

Web-sites:

http://www.hsus.org/pets/issues_affecting_our_pets/pet_overpopulation_and_ownership_statistics/us_pet_ownership_statistics.html

http://www.avma.org/reference/marketstats/sourcebook.asp

http://www.mybestfriendpettreats.com/

http://www.mybestfriendpettreats.com/

http://www.creativepetgifts.com/

Books:

U.S. Pet Ownerships & Demographics Sourcebook by AVMA (Paperback – 2002

Pet Sitting for Profit by Patti J. Moran and Michelle Boles

The Encyclopedia of Natural Pet Care by C.J. Puotinen

Healing Powers of Pets, the: Harnessing the Amazing Ability of Pets to Make and Keep People Happy and Healthy by Marty Becker

How to Start a Home-Based Pet Care Business, 2nd (Home-Based Business Series) by Kathy Salzberg

Pet Assisted Therapy: A Loving Intervention and an Emerging Profession--Leading to a Friendlier, Healthier, and More Peaceful World by Pearl Salotto

Dog Grooming For Dummies (For Dummies (Pets)) by Margaret H. Bonham

Best businesses to start based on this trend:

Mobile/Grooming pet care service

Pet baskets for birthday's, special occasions

Gourmet pet treats

Pet sitting services

Designer Pet Clothing

Pet walking service

Pet Funeral Services

Pet Photographer

Trend #15-Franchise Consulting

What's driving this trend?

For those of you who keep up with franchising trends, all you need to do is look around as you drive along a congested roadway to see the explosion in franchising opportunities. It's everything from Maui Taco to McDonalds to Dairy Queen! And those are just the restaurant related businesses. There are so many other areas to investigate that are not food related at all. They appeal to almost every need and offer a variety of opportunities for those interested in owning their own business. The popularity of franchise ownership has blossomed in the last decade due to the rough economy and downsizing from many companies. Franchising offers a viable alternative to burned-out executives looking for a fresh start in the world of business ownership.

Many of these executives have been downsized in the last several years and are looking for alternatives to corporate life. The interesting lure of a franchise is they take much of the risk out of the equation when starting a business. Think about if you were to start a business purely from scratch? You would have to design a business plan which would include a marketing plan, financial plan, distribution plan and a sales plan to name a few. Not to mention leasing a retail location and equipment if the business requires these essentials. The franchise route takes many of these unknowns out of the equation so that you don't have to think about how you're going to accomplish those tasks. When you buy a franchise, the business plan and all the necessary marketing and branding has been done for you.

Think about a UPS Store franchise. UPS has been in business for over 100 years. Don't you think they've learned a thing or two about delivering those little brown packages? When you open a franchise store, you don't have to market UPS the brand, it's already been done for you. You don't have to prove to your customers that UPS is good at delivering packages. They've done it for you. You don't have to pore over financial plans on how to make money in this business. They've done it for you. When you buy a franchise, you're paying for the intellectual capital that has already been invested into developing the business plan. Kind of like a "plug and play" type system. You pay them the franchise fee and you're ready to play! But, remember, there will be ongoing fees you will have to pay to the franchiser on an ongoing basis. The fees paid usually are based on a percentage of sales otherwise known as royalty fees. It's so important to read the fine print when you are researching a franchise opportunity. Knowing all the facts up front and what fees you are obligated to pay before you write the first check will make the experience a whole lot easier from the start. Franchise ownership can be enjoyable and profitable for those who enjoy the freedom of working on their own and where much of the risk has been calculated.

There is a tremendous need currently in the marketplace to consult with potential entrepreneurs interested in a franchise opportunity. The amount of franchise possibilities has exploded in the last 10 years. There are dizzying arrays of choices people can make among these various businesses. For the uniformed, it can be quite a daunting task. The need to educate and inform people is an exploding opportunity for small business people interested in this field. It is probably a bonus if you've been or are and entrepreneur yourself to help lend more credibility to your clients. A background in finance or accounting would also help as well. You see, in this type of consulting business, you want to be able to develop a trust between you and your customer. A client is going to want to know that you have their best interest in mind and that you will do the right thing for them. If you prove this to them, you will have a customer for life. I always believe that true success comes to those who truly put the needs of others before themselves. If you truly are in business to help others find their dream and realize there full potential, you will find success for yourself in the process. A very important fact I learned long ago and it still holds true to this day.

One of the most important factors to remember in this consulting venture is getting to know your individual clients. Each one of them will be unique and different in their own way. That, my friend, will be the very key to unlocking their potential. Getting to know their background, religion, marital status, experiences, skill sets, hobbies, to name a few will help you build a personality profile of what this person is all about. This will be invaluable to you as help them on their journey. Many people, you will come to find out, will want to do the latest and greatest hottest thing going in franchising. But the thing they miss is that whatever the hot thing is, it may not be the best for them overall. As a consultant in this business, you will have to be astute enough to steer people in the right direction and not let them get caught off guard by the latest attention-grabber. It will be a lot better in the long-run if you take your time and to give much thought to the right opportunity rather than the quick opportunity. Believe me, your customers will recognize this and you will be rewarded for your efforts in the long term.

You should certainly consider a database of templates and worksheets that help you determine a profile for your clients. By having these templates and worksheets, you allow the client to put in very important information about them. I know you are probably asking yourself, "Well, Dan, how do I get paid for all this work I'm going to be doing"? Well, there are a couple of ways to look at this. You could charge a fee upfront and include all this work in one set fee. Or you could create an a la carte menu that allows a potential client to pick and choose which services they would like. And then there is a third way, which is a little more risky, but may have the greatest financial reward. You become a representative for the franchiser. What happens in this scenario is that you recommend to your client several different franchises choices based on their personality profile. If they choose one of the franchises you recommend, you are paid a commission from the franchiser. You could ultimately represent as many franchiser opportunities as possible. There really isn't a limit. Actually, the more franchiser's you represent the better chance you have of making the correct connection with your client and their business objectives.

A major key to success will be to develop a database of templates that will allow you to capture and analyze all pertinent information necessary for you to determine what the person's personality profile is and which businesses might be appropriate for them. You can easily get some of these profiles through Meyers-Briggs and some of the other well-known personality type tests through a Google search. If you have a web site developed, you could easily have these forms available in PDF or word format for people to download, fill out and email them back to you. By having them available on your web site, you've made it very easy for them to gain access. The other piece of information you will need to have available is the franchise information. This information should be gotten directly from the franchiser and should include prospectus, financial statements, royalty fees and any type of experience required. What you have now is the two main pieces of information required for your database, which will be essential to matching an individual with the right franchise opportunity.

Your marketing campaign can target many different groups. One that I would recommend, that you might find surprising is people looking for work! Surprise! Think about it. What better target audience for those who are in transition. I myself, during one of my downsizing periods, seriously looked at franchising opportunities. I even met with a coach who helped me understand what franchising opportunities existed and which ones have fit my skills and experience. I was a very captive audience as I had the time and energy to look at doing something on my own. Remember, when you are laid-off and looking for work, you become very receptive to each and every possibility that comes your way. Franchising is certainly an option for people out of work.

To market to this group it may be worthwhile to attend many of the networking meetings in your community. I remember when I was looking for employment; I attended many networking meetings through the local churches here in Atlanta. And during my attendance, there were many speakers that came and spoke. Everything from motivational speakers to people looking for participants for paid survey work. It ran the gamut. I would recommend contacting the leader of the networking groups and meeting with him or her first and make your presentation and solicit feedback. Once you've agreed on the presentation delivery ask for a scheduled time to come and talk to the group. Make sure your pitch is clear and to the point and extol the benefits of owning your own franchise and how your consulting business can provide a level of value. Be prepared to answer questions and to provide follow up in the event you can't answer everything on the spot. It's better to say you will get back to them with the right answer than give them an incorrect one. Another key point is to make sure you extol the virtues of owning your own franchise. Many of the people in your audience may have given it some thought already, but just need a little push and a little bit more information to get them really interested. Your key role at one of these meetings is to educate people. You shouldn't be trying to sell them anything, but rather to inform.

You may also want to consider marketing your franchising consulting business to the actual franchisers. I would pitch this proposition in a way that explains the benefits to both you and the franchiser. Marketing to them the concept that you can help them garner additional sales will certainly be an attention grabber. State the position that by helping to educate potential buyers on the virtues of franchise ownership and by assisting them in choosing the right business you are ultimately getting them closer to making a decision and an eventual sale. If you position it within that framework, I will guarantee you will have success.

What skills are required?

A love of small business and a burning desire to see individuals succeed in their own small business is a key skill! If you have those two skills nailed, then you are way ahead of the game. Business Franchise Consulting will be a huge business catering to the retiring baby boomers. Many of these folks will want to start a business; however, many want the security of something that already established. And in many situations, they will gladly pay the start up and royalty fees typically associated with a start up. Another key skill that is a requirement is taking the time necessary to get to know your clients. Remember, these are people like you interested in living the American Dream. It's important to know something about them and what they are interested in. Knowing their likes and dislikes and areas of interest will be critical in order to connect them with the right business franchise opportunity. If your potential client believes you have their best interest at heart, you will never have a shortage of customers. They have to know that you will develop a partnership with them and that you will do your best to create the right fit between their needs, skills and talents and the right business franchise opportunity.

I would also highly recommend getting a thorough understanding of current franchise opportunities as well as what new possibilities exist as well. Being well informed when it comes to working with your customers is paramount to your success. Become an expert in your field and people will flock to you for answers and advice. If you build that reputation over time, you will become someone who people naturally gravitate towards for the right answer. The demand for this type of work over the next 5-10 years will grow exponentially with the growing ranks of retiring baby boomers. This restless generation will welcome the opportunity to roll up their sleeves and to do something on their own. Many of them will want to go the route of franchising as it lowers the overall risk associated with starting up your own business.

What are my start up requirements?

I would suggest looking into two Franchise Consulting services called, Entrepreneur's Source and Frannet. Both are services that help would-be entrepreneurs determine a plan on which Franchise opportunity would be right for them. They are both on a national level and really do a good job of trying to understand the customer's profile and how that best fits with a particular franchise opportunity. I think a good way to start would be to get involved in either one of these franchise-consulting businesses. It will be a good way to understand how to start off in this business and a great place to learn as you develop the skills necessary to be a franchise consultant.

Check out these additional resources to learn more about <u>franchise consulting trends</u>:

<u>Web-sites</u>:

http://www.franchising.com/

http://www.franchiseopportunities.com/

http://www.franchisedirect.com/

Books:

Franchising For Dummies (For Dummies (Business & Personal Finance)) by Michael Seid and Dave Thomas

Franchising & Licensing: Two Powerful Ways to Grow Your Business in Any Economy by Andrew J. Sherman

The Complete Idiot's Guide to Franchising by Jr., James H. Amos

Is Your Business Right For Franchising? By Jr., Ralph Massetti

Franchising 101: The Complete Guide to Evaluating, Buying and Growing Your Franchise Business by the Association of Small Business Development Centers and Ann Dugan

So You Want to Franchise Your Business by Harold Kestenbaum

What No One Ever Tells You About Franchising: Real-Life Franchising Advice from 101 Successful Franchisors and Franchisees (What No One Ever Tells You About...) by Jan Norman

<u>Best businesses to start based on this trend</u>:

Business franchise consultant

Business Broker

Financial Analyst

Small business consultant

Career Coach

Writer for Small Business Trends

Trend #16- Financial literacy for teenagers

What's driving this trend?

I think the main reason this could be so successful is the gap that exists today in educating young people amount money management. So many kids today are unaware about financial matters. Most of them don't really understand enough about finances until they are on their own and self-supportive. And most learn through trial and error. I think one of the primary reasons we have so many people with debt problems is because they are not taught early enough about the power of saving money or the bad things that could happen with credit cards. We are a nation of spenders and if we don't begin to educate kids about saving for their futures, I shudder to think what the future will look like for our young people.

How many kids in middle school do you know that can balance a checkbook or know how to read a stock analysis? How many of us for that matter was taught money management when we were children? If you're scratching your head and furling your eyebrow, be comforted by the fact that you are not alone. Parents of our generation and even today's parents don't really offer much today in the way of education on money matters for their children. It's just not something that gets discussed. I think one of the reasons is that discussions about money and finances are something that parents do when the kids are in bed or not around. It's a topic that most parents don't want to get their children involved in. It's considered taboo. Or not appropriate for children under a certain age. I just think that's wrong. No I'm not suggesting that you and your wife sit down little Mary or Billy and begin explaining to them your financial woes. First off, they wouldn't really care and secondly you shouldn't needlessly worry children about home finances. What I'm talking about is the education and training of children on basic finances.

Why do I suggest this? Take for example the many stories you hear of college age students who start their school at a college or university and who are ill-equipped to manage their finances or get trapped in large credit card debt because they didn't know enough about high credit card interest rates. It's a story that gets repeated over and over again as kids start out on their first job already in debt! Simply mind-boggling!!! No young adult should have to start out like that mired in debt on his or her first day on the job.

So, this ultimately asks the question, "Would kids benefit early on from financial management courses early enough in life to give them a healthy perspective on money management 101". I have to think so. Like anything else in life, the more you know about something, the better off you are. Imagine the possibilities if your kids were taught early in life the huge benefits of savings. Just doing that one simple thing over the course of 20-30 years can add up significantly. If they were educated early on about compound interest and 401K plans, what do you think we would be raising-you guessed it, a nation of savers and people who knew the value of a dollar?

In this country we sorely lack a comprehensive financial education plan for young people. Most kids learn about money and finances through trial and error. With something that important, should we leave it up to chance? I would think you would agree with me this doesn't make sense. I would think the need is there and it's just a matter of time before someone catches on there is a need and creates a program that helps educate young people on money and finances. The benefits would be well received by parents as well. No parent would their kids entering the real world ill equipped in the ways of handling money. If anything, parents don't want their kids to be a financial burden to them, as they get older. Parents certainly want well-adjusted kids who can support themselves once they are on their own. The education should start as early as elementary school. Currently, most public schools don't incorporate this curriculum into the classroom. And if they are not going to do it, that leaves lots of room for opportunity for budding entrepreneurs such as yourselves to start a business educating students on money and finance. I'll tell you the place I would start is with a book. Yes, I did say a book. It doesn't have to be a long book, but one that highlights the gap in education and why you see it as being an integral part of a student's education just liking reading and math. You will want to make the case strongly to parents to get their attention. If you have them sold, they will certainly get the message their kids to be more educated on money and finance. You can get the book published on one of many of the on-line book publishers available such as iuniverse.com or booklocker.com. By getting yourself published, you validate your credibility. The key will be to be able to market your book affectively. The two keys to success for a good book are the title and the marketing effort that goes in behind it. If you have an eye grabbing, get-your-attention title and a savvy marketing push for the book, I guarantee you will sell books.

You can garner attention for your book through newspapers interviews and or radio spots. Many would-be authors call directly to a local newspaper or radio station and set themselves up for some free press. Many times the newspapers have a section where they highlight new authors and it's the perfect spot for a new author. Once you're in print and you market the value your book brings, you will start to create a "buzz" about your offering. The phone calls will begin. Trust me.

Once you've published a book, marketed it and sold it, you know have a qualified entry into this field as an expert on teaching about money management for young people. What this in turn allows you to do is to set up other channels for revenue, such as speaking engagements, consulting and seminars. All of these vehicles allow you to get your message out, build awareness and sell your services. There are many speaking engagements such as public schools, Rotary clubs, Junior Achievement meetings, etc. that have the right audience to promote your services. You could even begin your own column in the local newspaper. And once you've established yourself at a public school system, there could be opportunity to set up after school tutoring or an elective class student could sign up for to learn more about money management skills. When you think about it, the possibilities are endless. When was the last time you saw an investing book written for a twelve year-old? My point is that it's a wide open filed to serve this market that will help educate young people on the importance of investing early in life.

What skills are required?

An elementary or middle school educational background would certainly be a good skill requirement. If you have a formal background as a teacher, it gives you a good set of tools to pursue this opportunity. As a teacher, you've already acquired many of the skills and experience necessary to get involved in teaching kids about good money management. Qualities like patience and persistent as well as the ability to take adult themes regarding money management and make those applicable to a younger audience will work out well.

However, don't be discouraged if you are not a teacher by profession. I merely made the suggestion, as it is a good first step. By no means is it intended to say that if you don't have a background in teaching that you shouldn't try this opportunity. If you like money management concepts and discipline and enjoy teaching children, then by all means, you should get involved. I like this opportunity because we definitely don't do enough education regarding this topic. It is an underserved market and we need more emphasis placed on it if we are to teach children to grow up to be responsible adults when it comes to money management.

What are my start up requirements?

I would probably start with some informal marketing to better understand what needs exist in your area. Discuss the possibilities of incorporating the program through Junior Achievement as part of an after school program with school officials, teachers and other education experts. You can also see about creating an easy to learn book about basic money management and investing. Make it fun and engaging. Talk to parents informally about the needs of kids today when it comes to managing finances. I'm sure they will be able to offer a lot of input. Attend PTA meetings and find out what programs are currently being offered and how you might be able to offer your programs to further help educate young adults on financial matters. You will be amazed at how much you will learn from these information-gathering sessions. If you are sincere and affable and concerned about a child's learning, people will be more than happy to share their experiences and thoughts with you. Who knows, you might even develop some partners along the way who share your desire to help children become more versed in matters of finance.

The key message in this section is to just get out there and do it! You've got great ideas and a passion for what you want to do. The key is to get others to think like you and build some momentum around your desires.

Check out these additional resources to learn more about financial literacy for teenager's trends:

Web-sites:

http://www.mymoney.gov/

http://www.jumpstartcoalition.org/

http://www.financiallit.org/

http://www.parenthood.com/article-topics/article-topics.php?Article_ID=6176

http://www.uen.org/financial_lit/student/kids_activities.shtml

Books:

Personal Financial Literacy by Joan Ryan

Financial Literacy for Teens by Chad Foster

The Secrets of Money: A Guide for Everyone on Practical Financial Literacy by Braun Mincher

Saving and Investing: Financial Knowledge and Financial Literacy that Everyone Needs and Deserves to Have! By Michael Fischer

The High School Student's Introduction to Financial Planning: What you need to know that they don't teach you in high school by John Garza, Allan Burns, Rene Lausen, and Andrea Ruygt

Financial Literacy in Adult Life by Sandie Schagen and Anne Lines

Best businesses to start based on this trend:

After school financial program for young adults

Supplemental Financial Service to public schools (course curriculum)

Service business to Junior Achievement on financial literacy

Book writer publisher for books focused on financial education

Trend #17-Credit Crisis among U.S. consumers

What's driving this trend?

Huge! There are huge opportunities in this area. This is and will continue to be one of the most significant problem areas for people who fall prey to the credit trap. Let's face it Americans live on credit. We love to carry debt! It's right up there with mom and apple pie. The average American today carries $8,500 in credit card debt and pays the minimum amount each month to pay it down. At an average of 18% interest it would take you 47 years to pay off the balance! That's insane! When you do the math, the interest payments on the balance far exceed the value and amount you paid for the items in the first place. The current U.S. government debt is around $53 trillion, which includes all debts and liabilities. The U.S. consumer debt (American's obligation today as taxpayers) is more than five times the U.S. debt at $9.5 trillion, which includes what we owe on mortgages, car loans, credit cars and other personal debt.

And over the last five years with interest rates at all time lows and jobs plentiful, we signed up for even more debt. It's a problem in this country of epic proportions. People really and truly don't realize how much it affects them because it's all they've ever known. They don't know any differently. They don't have a clue what that money could be used for such as investments, college education or retirement. They don't know, because they've never had any discretionary income to put toward these other things. All they understand is how to get deeper and deeper in debt.

I truly believe there is a tremendous opportunity to help educate and train people on how to do a better job of managing their finances. Courses, lectures, classes and consulting services that can be tied into and overall financial management course would sell well.
If you have a background in financial planning, then you've already established your integrity. It means that you have credibility in the field already and that you have experience with people with credit problems. I think one of the biggest areas for potential is with young adults and teens. It's at this stage of their lives where they need the most attention to education. Educating young adults hopes to insure they won't make similar mistakes as their parents did. Finding a way to reach young kids through after school programs or on-line courses through the Internet would do well to serve this market.

But your main market will continue to be your adult population. I wouldn't even put an age limit on it at this point, because I believe they all need some level of assistance. It might be hard to charge this group money, particularly because of the financial situation they are in. However, one way to get started is to offer a free seminar. You can then offer at the conclusion of the seminar a one-hour session on money management or have information material, such as a book or short readings that you could offer for a price as well. If these clients see value in the seminar, they will be more likely to buy something they can take with them and use repeatedly.

You may be able to find many of your clients through credit counseling services where they may be overloaded with cases and would welcome your offer to help. You should make contacts with the credit counselors locally and see if they would be willing to send you references. This is a great way to establish oneself and get your name and reputation in this space.

The statistics are growing in this country and the fact remains that many people are not paying enough attention to the problem of their mounting debt. What consumers need is education on how to successfully manage their debt and to how to spot the warning signs they are getting in over their heads. Managing their debt correctly would allow them to be better prepared for the future when they retire. Carrying too much debt will severely impact their ability to save enough for retirement.

What skills are required?

If you have good communication skills coupled with a financial background, you are off to a good start! The key here is being able to communicate with people and getting them to understand the importance of good financial responsibility. If you are an accountant by profession or a certified financial planner, these are skills that could lend themselves as a good prerequisite to credit counseling. Or you can even leverage your own skills as a good saver and manager of finances. If you've "walked the talk" and have put your financial house in order, that certainly gives you some solid credentials to counsel others.

Planning and budgeting skills all come into play as desirable skills when it comes to providing this service to others. Take inventory of what you've accomplished to date and then see how you can take those same skills and create a business.

And that's the key to many of the businesses I recommend in the book. If you've got life experiences in many of these areas, you automatically qualify as an expert. Don't underestimate the value of your personal knowledge of a particular subject. Remember, your knowledge will be greater that someone who is seeking your advice and counsel. So, don't think your experience is for nothing…it means a great deal.

What are my start up requirements?

If you have experience in credit counseling, then you've certainly got a leg up. If not, it's not a big deal as I mentioned before. Experience accounts for a lot. Your biggest start up requirement will be two-fold. First, you've got to get the word out that you are available for this type of work and that you have the credentials to back what you say. It's all in the marketing and the positioning of how you communicate your services to people in need of credit counseling services.

I would get set up in a spare room in the house and not incur the expense of renting out an office. You can be just as successful in your own "home office" at a fraction of the cost. Invest in a good computer system, fax and printer. I'd also develop a series of "budget spreadsheets" that could be used to set someone up on a household budget. They will be very useful and helpful, as people will learn more if they can see their actual income and expenses on one sheet of paper. It will help them to visualize just how they need to budget in order to keep from falling into debt.

I'd also check in with the local credit counseling services to establish a relationship and to let them know you are starting up a small business and if there is any cases overload, that you would be willing to assist were appropriate. I would almost bet that many of these agencies are well overloaded with cases and would be happy to transfer some of the work to you. If anything, it's worth checking into. You never will know until you ask.

Check out these additional resources to learn more about *credit crisis among U.S. consumer trends:*

Web-sites:

http://www.business-opportunities.biz/2003/05/08/how-to-start-your-own-credit-and-debt-counseling-service/

http://www.amerassist.com/tmc/Business-Credit-Counseling.aspx

Books

How to Start Your Own Credit and Debt Counseling Service by Quick Easy Guides

Managing a Consumer Lending Business by David Lawrence

Digging others out of debt; a local firm offers free debt counseling to small-business owners. (Wendy Burkholder, Consumer Credit Counseling Service of ... An article from: Hawaii Business by Jacy L. Youn

Best businesses to start based on this trend:

Credit Counseling and Debt Services Business
Offer credit counseling and debt service courses to high school students
Become and author/create a blog/web-site for people who suffer from high-debt
Write a book on how to avoid debt and live debt-free
Design and household budget kit and calculator the people can use to avoid debt

Trend #18 - Image Consulting

What's driving this trend?

Many of us read the headlines each day and if you are like me you are aghast at the amount of people either looking for work or getting laid off for the first time. It was just the other I read about AT&T laying off 7,000 people corporate wide and Bank of America another 4,500 layoffs planned. Those are huge numbers! The headline from AT&T and Bank of America typifies the paradigm shift of what is occurring in today's economy and it's the primary reason for me writing this book. And it's not a temporary phenomenon. The trend not to hire is not a trend at all, but reality. Companies have figured out how to do more with less. At New Balance each employee is producing 37 percent more sneakers than he or she did four years ago. At their company's factory in Maine, the time it takes to turn an order into a shipment has declined from three weeks to eight hours, all in the past four years. This is a dramatic improvement compared to four years ago. They will replicate this capability across multiple plants over the course of the next several years.

We are experiencing cataclysmic shifts in hiring practices across a broad range of U.S. companies. The last thing in the world a company wants to do is hire someone when you factor the training, healthcare costs as well as yearly salary increases to keep that person on the payroll. For those of you out of work currently and hoping for the days of jobs being in abundance, it's just wishful thinking. Hiring in today's job market has changed forever. Companies will continue to hire temporary workers and outsource as much as possible in the 21st century. It's all about saving cost and the quickest way for them to realize cost savings is to cut headcount. It's that simple.

But it's not all doom and gloom. If you are considering starting a small business in the near future, I think one that focuses on image consulting would be in demand. Remember, many of the out of work individuals have worked for the same company for many years and do not have a clue about looking for a job or dressing for success. It's becoming a serious problem. New job seekers that haven't had to look for a job in many, many years are at an extreme disadvantage. They need a lot of help teaching them how to network, how to land an interview, how to negotiate a salary, how to position their strengths and how to sell and market themselves to people responsible for hiring decisions. Competition has gotten extremely tough and employers have the upper hand when it comes to hiring and it's only going to get tougher. Candidates today need as much help as possible in terms of prepping and mentoring them on how to best position themselves to get and secure their next position. They have to be much better prepared than the next person due to the competition in today's marketplace.

If you are someone who understands how to market and position candidates for job selection and promotion, this could be a lucrative area for you to pursue. I believe there is a strong need that is not being satisfied. Many candidates spend a lot of time focusing on their achievements, skills and work performance, but many of them neglect how they are supposed to position themselves during the courting process you see, finding a job is a lot like dating. At first, you are on your best behavior, making a good impression and saying all the right things. You want to sell yourself! It's no different in a job search. You have to say and do all the right things during the interview process so you get second date or a chance to come back for a second interview. And if you come in with the wrong message and not say the things they want to hear or you are not dressed the part or don't' have an engaging personality and the know the power of marketing yourself, your going to find your resume in the round file; the trash. We all remember those first dates. And if you liked the person enough, you certainly wanted a second date, right?

I would suggest to get started in this business to frequent the job fairs, networking groups and your local Department of Labor. All of these locations have willing job seekers looking for any advantage at all to give them a leg up on the competition. I would recommend contacting the organizers for these events and seeing if you could meet with them for an hour or so and present your agenda and how your seminars could benefit the job-seeking community. If you do a good job of positioning your services you could become a permanent speaker at their meetings. Once you do get a time set and agreement on your agenda, I would focus on a very clear message: How to help job seekers in their overall image definition when looking for employment. This approach could touch many different components such as: effective resume presentation, networking, image consulting, marketing yourself, and positioning your skills and experience for maximum effectiveness. You could package these deliverables into a great presentation that shows all of these things working together in tandem and how they can get a person the results they are looking for when looking for a career.

The thing I like about marketing to the networking groups and job fairs is that you have a captive audience. People attending these types of meetings are going to be hungry for new suggestions and recommendations. To say the least, they will have an open mind to new ways of helping them in their job search. Their willingness to try different approaches will be high. When engaged in your first introductory session, make sure you key in the many areas they are struggling with such as: not getting return calls, stumbling on tough interview questions or not feeling prepared for an interview. This will help establish oneself as being in touch with their concerns and their pain points. You want to zero in on the areas that are causing the most concern for people.

Once you've been able to establish several clients, you'll want to schedule some time with each of them and getting to know them in terms of their personality, backgrounds, skills, experience, likes dislikes and hobbies to name a few. This will help you develop a personality profile on your client and to create a base to work from going forward. This information will be critical in order to get a complete understanding of the person's work history and personal vision and roadmap. A PVR is something we used quite often in corporate as it helped map a person's goals and vision to their talents and abilities. Many people go down a path in life mainly because they felt it was a good stable career that paid well while in college. They never really took the time to answer the question on whether it was the right fit for them overall and if it matched their talents and abilities.

And because of this, many people interview for jobs and careers that may or may not be the right fit for them. And because of this, they go into an interview unprepared, unmotivated and with little or no passion about the career. And you guessed it; an interviewer can spot this in an instant. Don't forget, many times an interviewer are looking for a fit and for enthusiasm from a candidate. Most people can learn a job, providing it's not a technical or professional job like a CPA. When a candidate lacks the motivation and doesn't "look" the part it's hard for them to give a good impression. It's important the candidate is going for the right opportunity in order for them to exhibit the right level of excitement. Trying to force fit this is a disaster waiting to happen.

If doable, your sessions with potential clients should take place in a professional setting. A professional consulting business such as this, would not work well from a home office. You will need a professional environment to conduct the interview and consultation. A big key to success with any client is going to be role-playing. This is one of the quickest ways to help a client move forward. Role-playing gets right to the heart of where the weaknesses lie and you can quickly assess how to overcome these areas and practice what you've learned live. You see, what you are trying to develop is a professional image for your clients. Developing this image comes across in many ways. A good positive image reflects positively on the employer and the person doing the interviewing. Most employers are looking for a good fit and someone who will blend in within the organization and get along well with others. The last thing management and human resources wants to deal with is a malcontent or someone who doesn't know how to get along with others. It's something many companies try to avoid at all costs and it all starts during the hiring process. That's why it's so important to project a positive impact from the very beginning. An employer or an interviewer will pick up on this right away and in a very short time-it takes someone literally 30-60 seconds to make up his or her mind about someone. So, you have a very limited window to make a first impression. That's why it's so important to go in with the correct image.

What skills are required?

A background in Human Resources, Professional Recruiting, and Sales Management are all good prerequisites to become an Image Consultant. All of these backgrounds allow a person to see first hand what potential employees are looking for in a prospective candidate. I know you're probably scratching your head on the Sales Management suggestion. But think about it for a moment. Sales professional are all about image, are they not? They have to be in order to establish rapport with their clients and get the sale, right? A background in sales is certainly one that would be very helpful toward establishing yourself as an Image Consultant.

You should really have a solid understanding of the entire hiring process end to end. It will help to understand what occurs during the hiring process at each step. Your job, as an Image Consultant, is to do exactly that, create an image for your client. Employers today are looking for the best that money can when they hire a new employee. Competition is fierce and HR scrutinizes this process a lot more than it used to years ago. A prospective job candidate needs all the help they can get including, dressing for success, understanding the company's background, products and competition as well as how they communicate the value they bring to a perspective employer. Most job candidates don't really take the time to do this thorough research. That's the gap you can fill as an Image Consultant.

What are my start up requirements?

Start your marketing campaign as soon as possible. The quicker you can get out there and make a name for yourself as an Image consultant the quicker you'll be able to establish a reputation. Finding places to speak and get engaged with employed and unemployed groups should be easy. You should be able to find support and network groups in your area through a Google search of job-networking activities in your area.

Your best way to create interest and a marketing buzz is to get out there and make a name for yourself. The more people get to know you, the faster you'll create name recognition and trust in your brand.

Set aside a spare room in your home for your computer, printer and for practice interviews. You'll want to create an environment that's conducive for people to feel comfortable and to engage in a mock interview setting. The more you can practice with an individual, the easier it will become for them to do well in a real job interview.

Check out these additional resources to learn more about image consulting trends:

Web sites:
http://www.aici.org/
http://www.fabjob.com/ImageConsultant.asp
http://homebusiness.about.com/od/homebusinessprofiles/a/bizidea_imgcon.htm
http://www.totalimageconsultants.com/
http://www.socialimage.net/
http://www.professionalimagedress.com/
http://ezinearticles.com/?A-Career-in-Image-Consulting&id=751

Books:

FabJob Guide to Become an Image Consultant by Tag Goulet and Rachel Gurevich
Image Consulting in the 21st Century by Brenda York-McDaniel
The Perfect Fit: How to Start an Image Consulting Business by Lynne Henderson Marks and Dominique Isbecque
The Winning Image: Present Yourself with Confidence and Style for Career Success by James Gray
Skinny Bits: Wisdom for a Flourishing Image Business by Lynne Marks

Flawless Consulting: A Guide to Getting Your Expertise Used by Peter Block

Image Consulting in the 21st Century by Brenda York-McDaniel

The Winning Image: Present Yourself with Confidence and Style for Career Success by James Gray

Best Businesses to start based on this trend:

Image Consultant

Writer/book publisher on importance of image

Image Trainer

Video Resume Service

Trend #19-Experiential Marketing for Small Business

What's driving this trend?

There is a book called " *The Experience Economy* ", Written by Joseph Pine and James Gilmore. The book, if you haven't already read it, is fascinating. It discusses the impact experiences will play in creating stronger and more individual relationships with consumers. Businesses must tie emotional as well as genuine experiences to build and sustain brand loyalty for their products and services. It's a must in order to survive in the future.

Delivering great service is no longer acceptable as a winning strategy. Demanding customer expectations, personalization and customized products will drive what customers expect and demand from a business. You must be able to differentiate yourself through experience.

Nike, Coca-Cola, Apple Computers, Heineken and UPS. Recognize any of these brands? Of course you do. They are known the world over and used by millions of people the world over. Some of these companies are over 100 years old and going strong. Why? In two simple words: Marketing and Branding. These companies understand what it takes to market as well as brand their products and how it impacts the consumer's perception. Brand recognition has taken on a whole new importance if you are considering launching a business today. It's due to increased competition and ease of entry. Many businesses today have a lot easier entry into the market and it's much easier to compete. Technology has allowed this to happen. What once was the domain of mainly large companies with deep pockets and huge budgets are now available for smaller companies as well. As a small business starting it's important to determine how you are going to separate yourself from the rest of the pack. Will you base your difference on value-added service, price, giveaways, and effective marketing campaigns? There must be something there in order for you to speed past the pack. You've got to think differently. How does a customer perceive your product? Are there other uses for it besides its intended use? How does the customer experience your product? Does your product make a statement about someone's lifestyle? Does it cross generations? Isn't Coca-Cola just sugar water when you get right down to it? But yet, they've been able to create a marketing campaign around the fact that Coke is not only a soft drink, but also a lifestyle. It has created brand loyalty envied the world over. Small businesses will need this advantage if they want to survive in this upper competitive environment.

In one of my earlier corporate jobs I worked for a company that manufactured corrugated boxes in which they sold to many well known consumer products companies. This company for the longest time was considered a hard line manufacturer and wanted to change its image to one that was marketing and consumer focused. In one of their division they developed a "Design Institute" that more or less resembled an n advertising agency. The intent was to create an atmosphere were creativity was encouraged and welcomed. Where customers could come in a collaborative environment to help redesign their packaging to reflect more of a consumer based company. The company that I worked for wanted to reflect this image through a technique called experiential marketing. Experiential marketing allows for your customer or consumer to become engaged in a collaborative fashion with the design and development of your products and services. Nike town is a good example of this type of marketing technique.

The power of marketing in today's economy is invaluable. I particularly enjoyed Sergio Zyman's book, "The End of Marketing as

We Know It". Sergio was Chief Marketing Officer at Coca-Cola for many years. He is a staunch believer in the power of marketing to generate sales. He clearly points out in his book that if you are not generating sales through your marketing efforts then you shouldn't do it. Marketing efforts must clearly show a path to increased sales. If you are a budding entrepreneur looking to start a new venture, you will be spending a lot of time and energy on your marketing efforts. Getting a new business recognized and off the ground requires a lot of marketing effort. You've got to create the buzz around your products, services and value. Consumers have got to know these things about your product in a very clear and concise way. If they have to think about it too long, you've lost their interest. And if you plan to start a marketing consulting business to help other companies, I think you've chosen a good business venture. You won't have a shortage of business at all! Remember, marketing is something that small business thinks of last. It's not a top priority for them when they are trying to launch a fledging company. They have so many other priorities such as sales, production, personnel and administrative. But marketing is one of the most pieces they overlook. Small businesses forget quickly that if they don't market, they don't sell. They forget the need to create the buzz around the product and to tell consumers why they need the product. Marketing, to me, is the difference between what reality is and what the consumer believes reality to be. You are creating a perception in the consumer's mind this product provides value, is important, I need one, and that I am better off for owning it. If you can create this mindset with the consumer, then you've succeeded at your marketing efforts.

Marketing your products and services in an effective way can be your most powerful sales tool. Marketing must not be an underestimated effort. One of the best ways to market your marketing services is to begin building a reputation with a small-devoted customer base. It's important to build a base of referenced customers so these initial customers can become you marketing arm. There is not a more powerful marketing tool than a satisfied customer. They alone will do more for your reputation and further sales than all the money in your marketing budget. This is the same kind of advice you can dispense to your client base.

The Merriam-Webster Dictionary lists the definition of marketing as such: 1a: the act or process of selling or purchasing in a market b: the process or technique of promoting, selling and distributing a product or service. 2: An aggregate of functions involved in moving goods from producer to consumer. And the American Marketing Association describes it this way: The process of planning and executing the conception, pricing, promotion, and distribution of goods, services and ideas to create exchanges that satisfy individual and organization objectives (AMA 1985). And last but not least, a description from the FiveTwelveGroup: "The activities of listening to customer needs, assessing the competitive landscape and then designing and creating products and services accompanied by messages that shape audience perceptions, leading to opportunities for revenue. The primary objective of marketing is to deliver products and services to the right audience at the right price and right time, thereby increasing brand loyalty". "Marketing is creating an awareness of our value"-L. Paul Ouellette, Ouellette & Associates Consulting, Inc.

Think about for a moment-Why does Marketing Matter? A person wakes up in the morning after sleeping on a marketed bed, in marketed pajamas. He or she will bathe, wash with marketed soap, shave with a marketed razor, have breakfast with marketed juice, cereal and toast which was toasted in a marketed toaster, put on marketed clothes and looks at the time on his marketed watch. He will drive to work in a marketed car, sit at a marketed computer, drink his favorite-marketed drink and write with his marketed pen. Yet this person hesitates to market, saying that marketing does not return anything for the dollar invested. And finally, when it's too late, and his contributions are outsourced-he will then review the opportunities that are being marketed to the jobless.

I often like to think of marketing in terms of the Ten Commandments. It gets people's attention. When you start you marketing and consulting business, it might be a good marketing idea to have these printed on the back of your business card. It's a great way to introduce yourself to a new client and begin with the basics of why marketing matters. Let's go through them:

1) Solving client business problems is our only business
2) Our clients are our purpose
3) We need our clients' business
4) Our clients are not changing our systems, they are enhancing our systems

5) Serving our clients is not a favor we offer, it is mandatory for our survival
6) Our clients are real people, not an imaginary stereotype we created
7) We don't argue with our clients, we influence them
8) Our clients have the requirements, we fulfill them
9) Our clients deserve a professional attitude at all times
10) Our clients are the conduit between us and the business we serve

It also might be prudent to have your client hang these in very visible areas throughout their office for all employees to see. Reinforcement of these beliefs on marketing is the best way to have the instilled in everyone in the business, not just the marketing department. And last but not least, I'll leave you with a simple but brutally honest mandate for marketing: Market or Die a Slow Death! And it will happen, trust me. The best advice you can give your clients is to never underestimate the power of solid marketing programs to drive sales and improve growth. So, go forth and market!

What skills are required?

First and foremost, a strong belief in marketing experiences to consumers and to create a once in a lifetime event that connects a person to the brand in a unique and fulfilling way. If you are able to understand the importance of this experience and market it to others, then you've got the foundational skills to become a consultant in this area. With an opportunity like this one, you've got to have a passion and belief in stepping outside a traditional role of delivering great service and creating truly memorable experiences for your customers.

A background in marketing and or sales would be a good fit to consult with small businesses on the power of experiential marketing. The concept too many small enterprises will seem foreign at first and it will take someone who is passionate and who beliefs in the concepts to get others to think the same way. You will be introducing a new way of thinking to people and it will take an individual who understands the benefits and value of experiential marketing.

What are my start- up requirements?

If you haven't read *"The Experience Economy"*, pick up a copy as soon as you can and read up on this interesting look at how consumers will buy from companies in the future. Do your homework when it comes to small businesses in your area and how they currently market their product and services. You will probably find that many small businesses today have not heard of the concept of experiential marketing.

You will also want to begin marketing yourself to these businesses that could benefit from getting consumers to "experience" their products and services. Align yourself with the local Chamber of Commerce and SBA in your area and get on their calendars for speaking engagements. You should also consider setting up a web site where potential customers can gain access to information, your availability and any publications you have that can help them become more educated on this topic. You can also post articles, research information and other topical information that will help your client base.

Developing and maintaining a web site today is almost mandatory if you are going to have a presence on the web. Today, many people first go to search the web for information on a particular topic of interest. If you do not have a web site constructed, you could be missing out on a lot of potential business.

The key here for start-up requirements is to get exposure in the market as an expert in this filed. Establish yourself as the "go-to" person regarding experiential marketing. You'll need to market your abilities, talents and passion. If you do that successfully, you'll be on your way!

Check out these additional sources to learn more about <u>experiential marketing trends:</u>

Web-Sites:

http://www.wisegeek.com/what-is-experiential-marketing.htm
http://www.adweek.com/aw/content_display/news/e3i6fbed77b64a1da5bcdf42cb82bc8438b
http://www.marketingwerks.com/

http://www.koganpage.com/products/experiential-marketing/MarketingandSales/M/Marketing/M001/1002649/9780749452759/

http://findarticles.com/p/articles/mi_m0EIN/is_2008_Oct_7/ai_n29481663/

Books:

The Experience Economy: Work Is Theater & Every Business a Stage by B. Joseph Pine and James H. Gilmore
Experiential Marketing: How to Get Customers to Sense, Feel, Think, Act, Relate by Bernd H. Schmitt
Experiential Marketing: A Practical Guide to Interactive Brand Experiences by Shaz Smilansky
Experience the Message: How Experiential Marketing Is Changing the Brand World by Max Lenderman
Truth: The New Rules for Marketing in a Skeptical World by Lynn B. Upshaw
Managing the Customer Experience: Turning customers into advocates (Financial Times Series) by Shaun Smith and Joe Wheeler

Best Businesses to start based on this trend:

Experiential Marketing Consultant

Interactive and Marketing Technology Business

Expert Speaker/Author on the subject of experiential marketing

Small-business experiential marketing consultant

Trend #20- Organic Health Foods

What's driving this trend?

Organic food accounts for less than 2 percent of U.S. food sales, but the industry is growing like a weed. Sales of organic food increased 21 percent between 1997 and 2002, according to the Organic Trade Association. Industry analysts expect sales to grow by about 20 percent annually in the next few years.

In general consumers today are looking for healthier alternatives to pre-packaged foods for both themselves and their children. There is so much information available today that discusses the negative side of pre-packaged food ingredients. Consumers today are a lot smarter and much savvier when it comes to the food the buy and prepare for their families. Food companies to day as well are under more pressure to list ingredients and substitutes in their food products. Starting in 2006, all food manufacturers will be required to list the amount of Trans fats contained in their products. Trans Fats are considered the bad level of fats know to cause heart related problems. It has been know for a while that many of the preservatives in foods that are included to help food stay fresher longer are harmful to us. People today are more conscious about the foods they buy and are demanding healthier, organic products. Over the last ten or so years, health food stores have begun to pop up in many neighborhoods across the U.S. Even many of the regional grocery chains have whole sections of their stores devoted to organic and healthy foods. This is a trend that will continue to grow as more consumers drive the demand.

Another key driver of this trend is the growing population of obese children. Children today are more at risk for adult related diseases such as high blood pressure, diabetes, and other heart related illnesses at an alarming rate. Parents are looking for solutions such as more exercise in gym class and better eating habits. They know that if they can educate their children on the benefits of eating healthy when they are young, the better chance they have of avoiding debilitating illnesses later on in life. I just read recently a start up company in Connecticut that provides healthy, natural meals prepared for day care age children and delivered directly to the day care. Many parents want to make sure they provide nutritious value in the foods their children consume. The Connecticut company makes it easy for parents to give their children healthy meals while they are at school. I am certain this trend will continue to grow, particularly with the growing rate of obesity among children. It has become a serious problem and parents are looking for answers to help their children maintain a healthy weight and to get more exercise.

What skills are required?

A background in nutrition and or food preparation services or both is a good start, but not the only prerequisite. It certainly helps to understand nutritional value and daily food requirements, particularly for children. It also helps to have credentials in the field as it provides parents with your qualifications as a certified nutritionist. It also helps to have good speaking and communication skills. Interpersonal and communication skills are critically important to create awareness on the importance on eating healthy. You could consider developing a newsletter or a web site to help let people know about your business. Educating a potential customer about the benefits of a product service is a better way to market that "selling them". People are more apt to buy something if they feel they are not being sold something. Educate them first and the sale will come as a natural outcome.

If you are going to market your service for healthy meals, you'll need to appeal to parents and school administrators to market the benefits and value nutritional meals provide. Getting your network established with school officials will help get you established with people that could help you within the school system. Public schools are coming under more scrutiny in the media today to provide healthier foods o school age children. The timing for a service such as your could be perfect!

What are my start up requirements?

Getting your network established should be first and foremost. As I explain in each of these sections throughout the book, it's vitally important to build a reputation as an expert. The earlier you can do this the better. People will respect you for your knowledge and will be more inclined to buy your products and services if they perceive you as an expert. You can start out small (which I highly recommend) by giving seminars and informative presentations on the benefits of healthy eating within the school lunch program. You can also make these sessions funny and engaging. People love to learn through example or through engaging and fun activities.

A lot will depend on your ability to make in roads into the school administration and to establish yourself within their network. The best way to gain ground in this field or any field for that matter is to build your network. Your best chance for success is to make a name for yourself and to establish your credibility and your reputation. You can start by writing some very informative emails to the school administrators about who you are your background, your goals and how you can be of benefit to both the school and the students. Ask for an informal meeting to come in and talk them about your nutritional program and why you feel it will have benefits to the students. Be ready with facts and statistics to back up what you say about the obesity problem in the U.S. today. You will certainly hit a cord with parents who are struggling with children who have a weight problem. Remember, parents want nothing more than what is best for their children. And their children's health will be of paramount importance.

Day care centers might be another way for you to pursue getting your message out about your nutritional services early on. Actually, the more I think about this option the more I like it. By marketing to the day care centers, you are appealing to parents who want to get a jump early on with teaching their children good nutritional habits while they are young. You could even venture into a prepared home meal delivery service similar to programs adult use when trying to lose weight. This could be a whole other opportunity for you to get in with organizations that have children as a wide audience.

So, hopefully in this section you've learned some valuable lessons on how to get started in this growing field. I do believe Organic Food Sales will continue to grow as more and more consumers opt for a more healthy choice in foods and lifestyle. Already, there are companies providing healthy food alternatives from snack and junk food through vending machines. Soon, sitting side by side next to the candy vending machine, you will see healthy snack food options for people on the go!

Check out these additional sources to learn more about the <u>organic health food trend</u>:

Web Sites:

http://www.consumerreports.org/cro/food/diet-nutrition/organic-products/organic-products-206/overview/

http://www.nytimes.com/2009/03/22/weekinreview/22bittman.html?_r =1&em

http://lookwayup.com/free/organic.htm

http://www.mofga.org/tabid/166/Default.aspx

http://www.grinningplanet.com/2005/12-27/health-benefits-of-organic-food-article.htm

Books:

To Buy or Not to Buy Organic: What You Need to Know to Choose the Healthiest, Safest, Most Earth-Friendly Food by Cindy Burke

The Organic Food Shopper's Guide by Jeff Cox

The Truth about Organic Foods (Volume 1, Series 1) by Alex Avery

The 150 Healthiest Foods on Earth: The Surprising, Unbiased Truth about What You Should Eat and Why by Jonny Bowden

Food to Live By: The Earthbound Farm Organic Cookbook (Earthbound Farm Organic Cookbk) by Myra Goodman, Linda Holland, and Pamela McKinstry

Best Businesses to start based on this trend:

Organic Food Store Operator

Owner/Operator Healthy Food Vending Machines

Organic Food Café

Kiosk Operator for Organic Foods

Organic Food Wholesaler/Distributor

Certified Nutritionist/Consultant to Public School System
Author/Writer on Best Practices for Healthy Life Styles

Motivational Speaker to Corporations and Health Clubs
Owner-Natural Health Food Store

Trend #21 The Mobile Workforce & SOHO (small office/home office)

What's driving this trend?

How and where American workers conduct business is changing rapidly. During most of the 19th and 20th century, many workers commuted to the office where they worked an 8-10 hour day and then left the office to begin their commute back home. Working from home, telecommuting and having flexibility during the workday during the normal 8 hour day were virtually non-existent. Much has changed in the last 10 years. More and more families are dual-income workers with children and are even responsible for aging parents requiring the need for more flexibility in their schedules. Technology has played a huge part in allowing workers to work from anywhere in a virtual environment. Technology is allowing companies to operate freely without worrying about geographic boundaries or international time zones. The workday in many parts of the world, due in large part by technology, has gone from an 8 hour day to one that is 24/7.

However, it does allow workers more flexibility to be in charge of their own schedule and not be so confined by such a rigid work schedule. The worker in the 21st century has a lot more flexibility to set his or her hours, work from home and spend more time with children and aging parents. Corporations as well are under pressure to conform to a more flexible schedule by employees. Because they have more demands placed on them on a day to day basis, they require their companies to allow them more flexibility and autonomy on how they schedule they work day. The net effect is that companies get a more satisfied and less-stressed worker if they can accommodate this type of flex-schedule work arrangement.

What skills are required?

For this trend, you could apply many skills and experiences you've learned to uncovering opportunities to serve this market. Many of these workers who telecommute and have flexible hours still don't have time to do many of chores and errands we are all required to do on a daily basis. Think about the services and or products people who work from home might need? What things are they not able to do themselves because of lack of time? What business service could you provide to help fill the gaps?
Well, for starters, many would need day care service for their children if they are not school age. Although a mom who's employed, and may work at home, she still may need quality day care to watch her children so she can concentrate on her job and responsibilities while working from the home office. And on the other side, you may have elderly parents living with their children who work from home. The

same applies here as well, finding a quality eldercare service that provides activities and social events for older parents. How about a laundry service that picks up and delivers to someone's home? How about a home delivery meal service? People working from home value their time just as office worker and would welcome the opportunity to utilize these types of services. If they are working from home, they don't want the added stress of taking care of children and aging parents while they are trying to work a full day at their home office.

Another key service for the SOHO market is computer training and networking. Almost every home business is going to have some level of technology needs. Whether it's setting up a wireless network, installing new software or new hardware, each SOHO worker will need help in this area at some point. So, if you are technically inclined and enjoy fixing and repairing as well as installing software, this could be a perfect market for you.

What are my start-up requirements?

Your first start up requirement is to first identify the need in this market. It's imperative to fill a need that's not being fulfilled. I've seen many businesses fail trying to fulfill a need that doesn't exist. Find the pain or gap in this SOHO market and create a valuable product or service that people will want to buy from you over and over again. The other critical component is to match the need with something you enjoy and are passionate about. I know this sometimes sound trite; however, it can be stated enough. If you are starting a small business other than it's because you really enjoy doing it, then what's the point. Really like something before you venture off and spend your hard-earned investment and time. Remember, if you love what you do, you'll never work a day in your life.

Once you've decided on a particular business idea to serve the SOHO market, you'll need to set up a comprehensive marketing program to reach your target audience. Keep your marketing costs low and do a lot of word-of-mouth advertising. Attend and speak at local Chamber of Commerce meetings. Get to know the local business community and create a name for yourself as someone who knows the SOHO business and has a value added product to provide to the market. You'll be amazed at how effective this will be in creating a buzz in the market about the services you can offer. The best advertising is sometimes the best through networking and just through people passing your name along and praising your work.

Check out these additional sources to learn more about SOHO trends:

Web-sites:
http://www.cioupdate.com/trends/article.php/3725551/The-Reality-of-the-Mobile-Workforce.htm
http://www.soho.org/
http://www.ceoexpress.com/links/bpsoho.asp
http://www.chiefhomeofficer.com/
http://www.toolkit.com/

Books:
The Home Office Solution: How to Balance Your Professional and Personal Lives While Working at Home by Alice Bredin

The Home Office and Small Business Answer Book: Solutions to the Most Frequently Asked Questions About Starting and Running Home Offices and Small Businesses by Janet Attard

Building the Custom Home Office: Projects for the Complete Home Work Space by Niall Barrett

Small Office Home Office (Architecture Details) by Marina Batlle Brugal

Best Businesses to start based on this trend:

Graphic Designer

Computer Networking Service
Laundry Service (home pick-up/drop-off service)
Home Meal Delivery Service
Child Day Care Service
Eldercare Service
Ink Jet Cartridge Home Delivery Service
Mobile Oil Change Service

Trend #22-Environmentally Safe Products

What's driving this trend?

The media has saturated us with news and information regarding the fate of the planet and how we have not been good stewards of our environment. Headlines which start out with the heading, "Global Warming" bombard us almost on a daily basis. Former Vice President, Al Gore's book, "An Inconvenient Truth" was made into a documentary and won several prestigious awards from Hollywood. Large and small companies are all making headway in creating products that are more eco-friendly and that don't pollute the environment. The auto-makers are bringing to market hybrids that run on alternative energy sources and solar energy companies are designing new and innovative products to reduce our dependency on oil and fossil fuels.

You can't help but see the constant media coverage of the country's concern or should I say obsession with the environment. Now, you can debate the fine points of how accurate the scientists and Washington bureaucrats are regarding the belief that humankind is somehow to blame for the gradual warming of the planet, but one thing is for sure that it certainly makes sense for us to take better care of our environment and to limit our dependency on foreign oil.

The trend is clear. We know as a nation we must take better care of our environment. This will create opportunity for entrepreneurs who understand this trend and who can capitalize on sound business ideas. There will be a growing need for products and services in this burgeoning market that serves an environmentally friendly marketplace.

What skills are required?

Understanding the marketplace for environmentally safe products and which ones would have the biggest impact with consumers. And that is not an easy task. You've got to have the ability to determine which direction the market is moving and be able to see how you can develop a product and or service that best fits. Timing will be a key component also. Doing a thorough job of marketing research cannot be underestimated. There is so much dialogue and discussion in the media today; you have to filter through what is real and what's not. The marketplace will, undoubtedly, get very crowded as entrepreneurs try to capitalize on this emerging trend. Some will be successful and some won't. The one's who do well will be the ones who understand their specific market niche' and do the appropriate homework. The key will be to not try and be all things to all people. Try and pick and stick with a particular area and do it better that anybody else. Look for areas the bigger, more established companies are overlooking or ignoring. That has always been the method of small, nimble successful companies; finding a need to fill the large companies have overlooked. And don't be afraid to experiment. This is such a new field; theirs is room for growth by trial and error. If you think a certain area is not were you should be, change course and pursue another avenue. The market is too big and too new to get stuck in one area of discipline early on.

What are my start-up requirements?

A thorough and knowledgeable understanding of the market you intend to pursue. If you do that successfully from the beginning, everything else will fall into place. Shortcutting the first step will have consequences throughout each phase of your marketing, product development and sales execution efforts. Know your market, your product and your customers better than anyone else. Don't overlook any type of government grants. Since many states as well as local and state governments may provide incentives for environmentally safe products, please check out what funds might be available to you. You may be very surprised to learn what might be available to you to help you get your business off the ground. There could also be some tax benefits/credits as well when you file at the end of the year. Check your federal and local government web sites as well and consult with a knowledgeable tax accountant who is familiar with these types of government incentives. Get out and talk to as many people as possible. It will be the best education you will receive. Most people are glad to help out when they see someone just starting out. It's a natural response to try and help were appropriate.

Check out these additional resources to learn more about environmentally safe product trends:

Web-sites:

http://www.solatube.com/dealer/atlanta.php?gclid=CKfKucTbvpoCFQKHxwod-wzhsA
http://www.aehf.com/
http://www.seventhgeneration.com/
http://www.envirosafehealth.com/biogreen/
http://www.ehow.com/how_2070438_buy-environmentally-safe-products.html
http://www.ecomall.com/biz/cleaning.htm
http://www.greenmercantile.com/
http://www.fiberclaycouncil.org/environmentally-safe-products.html
http://www.thediaperlady.com/environmentally-safe-cleaning-products.htm

Books:

Selling Dreams: How to Make Any Product Irresistible by Gian Luigi Longinotti
NATURAL HOUSE CATALOG: Where to Get Everything You Need to Create an Environmentally Friendly Home by David Pearson
Tuned In: Uncover the Extraordinary Opportunities That Lead to Business Breakthroughs by Craig Stull, Phil Myers, and David Meerman Scott
Phrases That Sell: The Ultimate Phrase Finder to Help You Promote Your Products, Services, and Ideas by Edward W. Werz and Sally Germain

Best Businesses to start based on this trend:

Environmental Learning Toys for Children
Home Cleaning Products
Decorative Rain Barrels

Home Gardening Kit for Organically grown products
Independent Consultant to business on "Green Initiatives"

Trend #23-Financial Investing

What's driving this trend?

If you like to keep up with current events and trend, like I do, then you can't help but notice all that is written lately of the baby boomer's lack of saving efforts throughout their lives. Now, for me, I basically take what I've read and cut it in half. Meaning, I pretty much believe only half of what I hear. Let's figure it this way. There are 76 million baby boomer's Half of that number is roughly 38 million people, have of that is 19 million people. You get my point; it's a big market! There are always going to be people out there looking to better their financial position, learn more about investing, how to budget their money, save for college, buy a home or even a car. Over the last twenty years, the percentage of people now invested in the stock market is 50%. And that was from a few years back. It may be even higher now. The difficulty people have today as in the past with investing and saving is because 1) They don't know where to start; 2) They lack the discipline; or 3) They are confused by all the choices they have. It can be so overwhelming to some they completely ignore the whole process and refuse to get engaged at any level. The people in the industry don't help matters by making it so confusing for people. When it comes to investing and saving for the future, sometimes simpler is better. A little money saved each month, periodically in a Roth IRA or 401K for example can grow to a large sum from the simple equation of compound interest. Time is always on your side when it comes to investing. That's why I encourage young people to start as early as possible. Young children have a much greater chance of becoming millionaires through steady investing principles over a consistent period of time versus winning the lottery or becoming a professional athlete. Yet so many people miss this opportunity.

I am almost certain that if parents taught their children early in life the value of investing and saving from a very early age, there wouldn't be these issues when they grow to be adults. People learn at a young age the difference between savings and spending. If we have role models, such as parents who spend all of their money and don't save it, that's the model we learn to live by. If, on the other hand, we grow up with parents who were good savers and planned and budget their money, we grow up to be good stewards of our money and learn to save and budget correctly.

There is great opportunity in the area of educating people, young and old, on the merits of good financial planning in this country. We have long been a country of excess and living beyond our means. And we are bombarded daily with credit card offers to obtain yet another credit card so we can get ourselves further in debt. Credit card companies target young people as well in high school and college trying to entice them with their own credit card, knowing the earlier they start charging, the more inclined they will do it as adults.

What skills are required?

A good solid knowledge of the financial markets and how to work with people on getting them set up on the right path to save for college education expenses and their retirement. Essential, to this skill set would be someone who completely understands all the required components of good financial planning, such as proper life insurance coverage, risk or appetite for different investments vehicles like stocks, bonds, mutual funds, cash, and proper time horizons based on age and risk. If you have a bit of sales in your background, that helps as well. Most people, when it comes to planning and budgeting for their future are not always willing to take the time to site down and actually plan. If you possess the skills of persuasion and are able to point out the merits and value of good financial planning, you will be much more inclined to "sell" your clients on your services.

And lastly, on a personal skills level, you have to like working with people and have enough patience to let people make their decisions without feeling like you have to apply pressure. Most people will not want to rush into making these sort of decisions and will need time to understand everything they are looking to do If you have the willingness to be patient and stay with your clients during this process, you will be a reputation as someone who understands and cares about your clients, rather than someone just looking to make a quick sale.

What are my start up requirements?

One of the key start up requirements will be clients. It will be important to build a steady flow of repeat customers that want and need your service. There are several ways to approach this. One way is to get your name out there to the public through speaking engagements at business meetings, rotary club and small business forums. By speaking at these types of functions, people get to see and hear your level of experience and you establish instant credibility. You also get a chance to build relationships face to face and one on one. There is absolutely no substitute for clearly getting to know someone and building a trusting relationship. You cannot put a price tag on that kind of marketing.

It also might make sense to build ties with area CPA firms who could easily refer you to potential clients. CPA's stay very busy with client tax needs and can refer you to their clients who might need financial planning services. You may also want to consider "free seminars on financial planning offered through the CPA firms as well. Mention the word "free" and you will definitely attract a lot of attention. I'm a firm believer in marketing to clients through education and consulting to show them value before you begin to charge for your services. It's much easier to begin charging for your work if people can see the true value and benefit.

Check out these additional sources to learn more about *investing and financial security trends:*

Web-sites:

http://www.practicalmoneyskills.com/

http://www.fdic.gov/CONSUMERS/CONSUMER/moneysmart/

http://www.jumpstartcoalition.org/

http://www.financiallit.org/

http://www.financialeducatorscouncil.org/

http://www.submityourarticle.com/articles/Vince-Shorb-2822/youth-financial-literacy-programs-63582.php

http://hbswk.hbs.edu/item/6093.html

http://uanews.org/node/19954

http://www.newyorkfed.org/newsevents/speeches/2001/stw011201.html

Books:

Financial literacy is making a comeback. (Curriculum Update): An article from: District Administration by Ellen Ullman

How Much Is Enough? Making Financial Decisions That Create Wealth and Well-being by Arun Abey and Andrew Ford

Smart Women Finish Rich: 9 Steps to Achieving Financial Security and Funding Your Dreams (Revised Edition) by David Bach

Money Sense for Kids by Hollis Page Harman

Smart-Money Moves for Kids by Judith Briles

Kids Finance 101: A Guide to Financial Success for Parents and their Children by Yvonne Brooks

Growing Money: A Complete Investing Guide for Kids by Gail Karlitz

Dollarsmart Resource Guide for Kids: A Comprehensive Financial Education Guide for Parents and Teachers by Cheryl Gorder

Who's Afraid To Be a Millionaire: Mastering Financial and Emotional Success by Kelvin E. BOSTON?

Best Businesses to start based on this trend

After school program or Summer Camp for Financial Education

Financial Planning Service

Financial Planning Services in inner cities

Writer/Author on Financial Planning Education

College professor of Financial Literacy

Radio talk-show host dedicated to Financial Education

Mobile Financial Planning services to rural areas

Web-site developer that helps people learn about financial literacy

Maker of board games that help teach financial independence

Trend #24-Home & Business Security Services

What's driving this trend?

The need for effective security systems has grown tremendously over the last six years, due in large part from the September 11, 2001 attacks on our country. Businesses, home owners, government all have a vested interest in improved security for their operations and the safety and protection of their employees. Unfortunately, we live in a world that demands that we take better precaution when it comes to protecting lives, important information and property. What does this mean for the small-business person or entrepreneur? It means greater opportunity, of course. After 9/11, the government created an entire agency called the Office of Homeland security whose sole focus is to protect U.S. citizens from foreign and domestic terrorism. This major shift toward enhanced security has created business opportunity in both the public and private sector. Many branches of government, including the military will look to the private sector to help them with their security programs. And if you happen to be on a preferred vendor list for these agencies, you could be bidding on multiple government contracts. You can even find vast possibilities in the private sector as well. Many parents who enroll their children in daycare centers during the day while they work are looking for more security in knowing their children are safe, happy and healthy during the day. Many centers have begun to install security cameras so that parents through the use of a webcam can view their children during the day without impacting their work day.

And businesses of all types, big and small, looking to protect sensitive information such as employee information or physical assets will look to security businesses to help them protect and preserve vital information and high-value inventory and equipment. The area of protecting sensitive employee and customer data is extremely critical. Many small to medium sized businesses don't have a way to manage their "paper documents" and still rely on the file cabinet method for storage and retrieval. This poses huge risk as the documentation to vulnerable to theft, fire and misplacement. Technology has allowed many larger businesses to take advantage of document scanning and document management systems to better handle the mountain of paper work businesses have to deal with on a monthly basis. These systems allow for better security and retrieval and give businesses a level of security they didn't really have operating in a manual, paper-driven environment. Alongside document management, is the need for document shredding or destruction of sensitive information. Again, many small businesses don't have a way to destroy documentation in a cost effective manner. Many businesses may soon be regulated to manage documentation at a more secure level and to also effectively rid themselves of sensitive information effectively.

What skills are required?

The skills required for pursuit in this field are really no different than many of the other businesses I've recommended. There are three main skill areas a small business starting out would need to focus 1). Conducting proper research and study of the security marketplace. I can't stress and emphasize this enough. Success or failure will be determined at this level. It's important to conduct a thorough marketing study to understand where the opportunities might be, who are your customer's, what products and services do they desire, what price do I charge and how do I deliver them in the most cost-effective way possible. 2) Understand your customer's requirements. If you try and build solution X and your customer wants solution Y, you haven't listened to what your customer is saying. Listening to your customer and understanding what their "business pain" is, is absolutely critical. Let your customer drive your service and product development. Your customer is going to be your best marketing department as they know what they need better than anyone. 3) Provide superior customer service. Once you've got the signed contract, the work is just beginning. You've got to execute and deliver on what you've promised. And if you do it successfully, you'll have a customer for life. Remember, it's more difficult to cultivate a new customer than it is to create a new one.

One of the most important skills you'll need is the ability to go out and talk to people about this business and the market. Your biggest asset will be your ability to market yourself and to create a sense of credibility to new customers. Research information regarding government contracts and see how you might be able to bid on these and become a preferred vendor. You'd be amazed at the many programs the government has to offer both from a subsidy standpoint as well as government contracts you might be able to bid on. A technical background will help in many ways as many of the small business opportunities suggested in this section could require someone who knows the technical side of designing, installing and testing security systems. It's not a requirement, however, it does help. You'll find that some or most of the work require to install these systems can be contracted out to 3rd parties. If you do contract this work out to a 3rd party, make sure you stay involved in the process from start to finish. If something goes wrong, your customer will be looking to you for answers, not the 3rd party contractor.

Please don't underestimate any training you will need to become successful in this business. Technology needs as well as products and services change rapidly in this field and you want to give customers the benefits of your knowledge, training and expertise.

Customers are always willing to pay a premium for excellent service at the right price. Make sure you are keeping current with the latest technology and products and get the right training and certification as appropriate.

What are my start-up requirements?

One of the best ways to get started in this business is to gain knowledge and experience by working for a similar business or competitor. This has many advantages. You will not only learn the business, gain skills and understand customer needs, but you will also gain insight into what works and what doesn't work. In other words, you will have information as to what needs are not being met in the marketplace. You can in turn, once you start your own business, use this data as a competitive advantage.

I would also recommend getting any and all training required to enter this field. Credentials such as degrees and technical certifications will make you credible in the eyes of your customers. There is nothing worse than being turned down for a potential project because you don't have the right credentials. Research as much as possible what training you will need so it does not become an issue. You will be glad you did.

Check out these additional sources to learn more about security services trends:

Web-sites

http://www.security-kits.com/

http://www.dsc.com/

http://www.supercircuits.com/

http://www.sunsecurity.com/

http://community2.business.gov/bsng/board/message?board.id=SelfEmployedHomeBased&message.id=132

http://www.hueandcry.com/northern-california-oregon-security-systems.php

http://www.workathometruth.com/

Books:

Affordable Security: A Do-It-Yourself Guide to Protecting Your Home, Business, and Automobile by Steven Hampton

Surviving in the Security Alarm Business by Lou Sepulveda

Securing Home and Business: A guide to the electronic security industry by Erwin Blackstone and Simon Hakim

Have You Locked the Castle Gate? Home and Small Business Computer Security by Brian Shea

The Complete Guide to Personal and Home Safety: What You Need to Know by Robert Snow and Robert L. Snow

Home Security, Second Edition: Alarms, sensors and systems (Newnes) by Vivian Capel

Best Businesses to start based on this trend:

Small-business security consultant

Document Management System specialist

Home & business security and surveillance systems

Security auditing professional

Designer of customized security systems

3rd party installer/technical specialist

Professional "code-breaker" (to test businesses vulnerability to hackers)

Trend #25-Energy Efficiency

What's driving this trend?

The U.S. continues to spend billions of dollars on foreign oil, increasing our dependency in the Middle East. However, the tide seems to be turning as the awareness on the environment has taken center stage and the Unites States focuses on ways to improve the way we develop alternative energy sources. The trend is clear and the opportunities in this space abound for small businesses ready to provide goods and services to this growing marketplace. I read an article just the other day about a couple of entrepreneurs looking to create and develop a "fan system" that sits above major interstates across the U.S. to capture the wind velocity caused by passing cars. They did do a quick study to say the energy created would be equivalent to 9,600 kilowatt hours or a savings of $800.00 dollars per year. Not enough to get the attention of venture capital firms, however, but you can see the trend and the willingness and the innovation entrepreneurs are willing to put forth to find solutions to the growing energy crisis in the U.S.

One clear driver of this trend is the media. They have certainly created headlines regarding this issue over the last several years. Politicians, namely Al Gore, has taken this issue and written a book, *Earth in Balance* as well as documentary movie, An Inconvenient Truth

What skills are required?

The focus on energy and alternative sources of fuel are going to be a big focus in the next several decades. Government mandates and requirements will help push this industry and create many opportunities for entrepreneurs. This is a very big trend for the future. I'm not sure if there is any one skill set or list of requirements that will prepare anyone to meet the challenges and needs of this marketplace. Skills acquired in other areas and disciplines will certainly help in the energy sector as many of the same skills needed for other industries will be need for energy as well. One thing I would recommend is to begin educating oneself on this market and potential businesses. It's important to separate the truth from fiction. I firmly believe you have three major thrusts in a new and emerging sector, the innovators, the imitators and the idiots. The first category will be the one's leading the breakthrough technology and literally pointing the masses in the right directions. The second category will find the ways to make the technology profitable and will be able to market it to the mass consumer and create sustainable business models. The third category will be in it for short term profit and the quick exit strategy. There is so much available information today on this subject that you should be able to separate the truth from the fiction. Since it is such a new field, you are not tied or limited to doing things a certain way or locked into a specific model that has worked before as this industry is being created as we speak.

What are my start-up requirements?

I always like to recommend to clients looking to start a business is to have some experience in the business you are trying to start and market. It doesn't have to be specific work related experience. It could be a passion or a hobby about a particular or desire. For instance, with Energy Efficiency, did you do things around your own house to save money through energy efficient means? Did you see a savings on your utility bills each month based on what you did to conserve heat or your air conditioning? Did you research solar paneling or other natural ways to save money on your current utility charges?

These are the type of things that would lend credibility to you as a seller of these types of services to prospective customers. If customers feel and understand that you've "been there, done that" they are more likely to believe you and buy your services or products.

Check out these additional sources to learn more about energy efficiency trends:

Web-sites

http://www.makeyourbuildingswork.com/make-your-building-work/operate-more-efficient

http://www.business.gov/manage/green-business/energy-efficiency/get-started/tax-credits.html

http://www.greenbiz.com/business/research/report/2006/07/07/energy-efficiency

http://smallbiztrends.com/2009/12/free-money-for-energy-efficiency-upgrades.html

http://www.delcotimes.com/articles/2010/04/30/business/doc4bdb0603cfb46170240799.txt

http://www.windpoweringamerica.gov/small_wind.asp

http://www.nyseg.com/UsageAndSafety/usingenergywisely/eeps/smallbusiness.html

Books:

Wind Power, Revised Edition: Renewable Energy for Home, Farm, and Business by Paul Gipe

Consumer Guide to Home Energy Savings (Ninth Edition) by Jennifer Thorne Amann, Alex Wilson, and Katie Ackerly

Energy Shift: Game-Changing Options for Fueling the Future (Future of Business Series) by Eric Spiegel, Neil McArthur, and Rob Norton

PERFECT POWER: How the Microgrid Revolution Will Unleash Cleaner, Greener, More Abundant Energy by Robert Galvin and Kurt Yeager

Profiting from Clean Energy: A Complete Guide to Trading Green in Solar, Wind, Ethanol, Fuel Cell, Carbon Credit Industries, and More (Wiley Trading) by Richard W. Asplund

Best Businesses to start based on this trend:

Energy Auditor/Consultant to businesses/residential on Government Energy credits

Researcher/writer for energy savings for home and businesses

Installation services for solar panels, windmills, rain collection conservation

Chapter VII: Controlled risk taking coupled with Innovation

Did you ever hear the expression, "Youth is wasted on the young", the saying is supposed to give you awareness that people who possess youthfulness, don't always have the wisdom and experience to understand and capitalize on opportunity. But then again, part of being young is to not be burdened with all the trappings of adult life with all its responsibilities and maturity. That's why being young and innovative is a perfect recipe to start something new and exciting in a small business. Youth has two major advantages...time and energy. That's why I think it's so important for young people to experiment with innovation and controlled risk-taking in their youth. There is a reason why so many universities and colleges have entrepreneurial programs available for graduates today. It's because young people want it as an option for a major and because young students realize there is no better time to create a business as society and the economy reward innovation and risk-taking.

Now, folks that are my age don't get your knickers in a knot and don't feel left out! There is still time for older entrepreneurs to get involved, it's just that your approach might be a little different, that's all. My recommendations in the previous chapter can be well suited to folks that are established and want to start something on the side or who are in transition and are starting a new business for the first time. So, see, there is something in here for everyone!

The list is endless of young entrepreneurs who started out in college or even dropped out of college to pursue their dreams: Bill Gates, Michael Dell, Jeff Bezos and Fred DeLuca to name a few. You probably recognize the first three, as their names are automatically recognizable. Fred DeLuca is the owner of Subway. He started his first subway shop in the late 1970's in Milford, CT and the rest is franchising history. But the one thing in common is they were young, innovative and they took risks. By its very nature, you have to have those three qualities in order to achieve success. As I mentioned before, society rewards those that exhibit those qualities and make good on their dreams.

I believe these types of behaviors need to be fostered in young people. And I think it's doable. Young people today don't believe in the same paradigm that our generation was fed: school, job, and security. Young people today look at that and laugh. They know it's not true anymore and that believing it will only lead to insecurity in many instances. They know they have to be innovative, think outside the box and try new things. It's the only true way you are going to be successful and create a level of security for yourself.

How do young people develop this taste for innovation and controlled risk-taking you might ask? Well, to be honest, some will have it as a natural-born skill and others could develop it and others might not ever develop it, which is ok too. I do think we need to do more in terms of educating and teaching young people these survival skills. And they truly are survival skills. Teaching young people independence and how to create and innovate in life to me are always good skills to acquire. Ideally, you would like to see this type of skills training being offered in the schools, but I don't think we will see that in our lifetime. Traditionally, the public school systems will continue to teach their core curriculum. This is how the state infrastructure is set up and that is how states, schools and students get measured. It's not going to change anytime soon. However, there are other ways to help instill innovation and control risk-taking skills. One of the easiest places to start these discussions is in the home. Think about it for a minute, what better place is there to get your child's attention? They could be simple, easy talks about entrepreneurs that are easily recognizable. Or things they have done in school that foster innovation such as school projects, assignments and homework. You can begin to make the connection with them and how they have already exhibited these skills. You may also want to encourage them to start a small business on the side. If they are younger, perhaps a lemonade stand or have them make up fliers for odd-jobs in their neighborhood. I read an article recently about a young man who started out this way in high school and now operates a business helping schools maximize their fund-raising activities and to keep more of the money they earn. There are countless ways to have young people get involved in activities that help foster this behavior.

Junior Achievement is another way to get them involved. JA mainly sponsors programs through local communities and public school programs where they come in and teach a lot of these skills I mention. It's an organized group that has developed methods to educate and train individuals on small business and entrepreneurial skills. I am signed up to begin training sometime after 2005. I'm looking forward to better understand how JA can provide these tools to help young people learn to innovate and take risks.

I can tell you from experience that innovation and risk taking is even rewarded in some of the biggest companies! Hard to believe, isn't it! Companies look to smaller businesses for innovation and creativity in many instances. Larger companies often lose the ability to be innovative because of their sheer size. That's why they seek out smaller and more creative companies to help them with marketing, sales training and product development. There are companies that are currently being established that deal only with the leveraging of intellectual capital. Let's say for instance a company was looking for a way to design a new product or service. An intellectual capital company could be used in this instance to help with idea generation, design and deployment. The client company could even buy or lease these ideas from these companies as well. You can begin to see why innovation and creativity play a pivotal role in establishing a new venture and what the market would be willing to pay for such a service.

A key area for innovation is within a niche market. This requires going into an area that most of the bigger companies ignore or don't find profitable. Most big companies don't cater to the smaller markets and this in turn opens up huge opportunities for smaller companies. Smaller businesses, the one's that can innovate and be creative can find ways to serve this markets overlooked by the bigger players. Niche markets offer an opportunity to make money as well. Many times a fledgling business will try to be all things to all customers. And a lot of times this isn't a great strategy. You become mediocre at many things, but never delivering a stand out product to a specific need.

I found a company a few years back called Big Idea Group that deals directly with inventors and entrepreneurs who have an idea, but who are unsure about its commercial viability. The Big Idea Group can help you determine if your idea has merit. They do this by working directly with large manufacturing and consumer products companies. They understand the needs in the market place and then match those needs with innovative products and services. The beauty of the program is that it doesn't cost the inventor money up front to get your idea reviewed by Big Idea Group. If your idea is one that has potential, Big Idea Group will work a deal to pay you for the idea and royalties going forward. I am a huge supporter of these of companies as they provide struggling entrepreneurs and inventors a way to get their ideas noticed and to test the waters to see if their product has money-making potential.

Other ways to foster innovation is to create an intense awareness regarding your surroundings. You may think that all the great inventions and innovations have already taken place in your lifetime. Simply not true! There was a woman local here in Atlanta that came up with a toe-less panty hose design that she successfully markets. She apparently got fed up with the uncomfortable ness of standard pantyhose and experimented with a new design and ultimately struck a niche that wasn't being served in the market. She recently appeared on the reality show "The Rebel Billionaire". I personally find newspapers and other articles in business publications and other media information to be good sources of innovative ideas. I read an article the other day that many baby boomers are ill-prepared for retirement. Not so much from a financial standpoint, but from the emotional side. Many are not ready to have all this time on their hands and they quite simply don't know what to do with themselves. The article went on to say this market is currently not being served! The light bulb went off and I began to think of several opportunities to satisfy this need. It's important to be aware of your environment and to try and see what others don't. What hidden possibilities exist to satisfy a need? What needs are out there that aren't currently being met?

Think about how many products you use today that you weren't using yesterday: eBay, cell phones and video games come to mind. Products such as these didn't even exist to a great extent fifteen years ago. Or how about Velcro or the Post-It note? Having small children myself, I can't begin to say how convenient it is to be able to slip my son's shoes on using Velcro instead of tying them each time! And Post-It notes have been a business staple in offices around the world! And I see potential in many new and exciting areas, particularly in technology to help the elderly and aging population. Soon we will have robots devices helping in the home of the elder generation. Many of these older people will not need to be in a retirement home, but could use some extra help with housework, cleaning, companionship and to help with taking their medication. This is where robots can fill that void! We already see it happening with Honda's Asimo robot or the Roomba vacuum cleaner that automatically cleans your rugs and floors.

Changes in demographics, population, age, economics, tastes and immigration to name a few all have an impact on innovation. If you are able to create an acute awareness regarding these changes and to stay attuned to what is going on around you in your environment, you will most certainly uncover opportunities. I believe the key to success in this area is to focus on a niche. A definition that works for me: "finding and filling a need for those areas that are currently not satisfied by anyone else". It really is a simple formula.

Many companies today are looking for this level of innovation among its employees. There is currently a gap emerging in the state of Massachusetts between innovation and job creation, as the state's high-tech workforce continues to shrink despite the growth of a robust technology infrastructure. The Governor of Massachusetts, Mitt Romney is calling on businesses to take advantage of innovations to create jobs and said state government needs to create a more entrepreneurial climate. The Massachusetts High Technology Council states that higher education must play a more important role in keeping the state competitive. The state's political, academic, and industry leaders must continue to act collaboratively to develop a technology-based economic plan for Massachusetts that will lead to economic growth. The state of Massachusetts has always been an area that embraced innovation. You can see from this information that U.S. states are looking to foster this innovation and turn it into job creation. They realize how vital it is to their economic prosperity. Innovation, in today's global economy, is a piece of intellectual property that is traded in an international market much like any other set of goods. Innovation in of itself is not a key to success. *Innovation must be turned into real products, satisfying real demand in the marketplace.*

Whether you are looking to innovate for yourself and for your small company or you're looking to help foster innovation in other companies, there is a roadmap to follow that will help guide you through the necessary steps to success. For me, successful innovation starts with leadership. An organization must be fertile, flexible and empowering. It must be willing to tolerate risk, welcome ideas and foster positive energy. The way it enables this is through leadership. A couple companies come to mind when I think of innovative leaders: Harley-Davidson and Chrysler Corporation. Many of you remember Lee Iaccoa in the early 1980's leading a turn around of the carmaker and working with the U.S. government for a guaranteed loan to help keep the company away from bankruptcy and away from hungry creditors. You may no think of this scenario as innovative, but from a leadership standpoint, Iaccoa was "innovative in his approach on how he would eventually save the company. Harley-Davidson has a long history of innovation. This 100-year-old U.S. motorcycle company has led the pace with innovative motorcycles coupled with an unparalleled marketing and sales program. Harley, in my mind, leads the charge when it comes to brand loyalty. It pulled itself up by the bootstraps from its parent AMF in the early 1980's and creates one of the most recognized brands in the world. Out of 300 original motorcycle companies in the early 1900's, it is the only one left standing besides Indian. Harley-Davidson is noted for its v-twin engine, unmistakable sound and styling that many brands try to imitate to this day. Its innovation and brand loyalty is what keeps this company strong and its stock price consistently in the mid-1950's.

Another innovative company that comes to mind as I write is Apple Computers. Steven Jobs has to be one of the most significant technology innovators of the 21st century. Apple's latest introduction, the iPod, is seeing sales go through the roof. Jobs saw the potential for technology and entertainment and married the two for a wildly successful product. I am more than confident there will be many iPod's sitting under the Christmas tree this season. The reason I reference these three companies is their leaders fostered this behavior. They nurtured it and made sure everyone in the organization understood that innovation was of prime importance to the company's survival. These leaders knew that without an innovation, risk-taking spirit they would be like everyone else…a commodity with the same old products and technology. Another trait of innovation is looking at the world as your customer. Think and dream big! I remember being a child and having my parents tell me that reaching for the stars was a noble pursuit, because even if you fall short, you would have still attained a significant milestone. If you limit your reach, you'll limit your marketing and sales potential. The power of technology, particularly the Internet is a great way to look "big" to prospective clients and customers. Small businesses and start ups can look just like their bigger counterparts thanks to technology. The Internet breaks down walls and barriers to doing business and gives you a much broader reach beyond what you can imagine. On-line businesses such as eBay and Amazon.com are perfect examples. Each of these businesses is not hampered by geographic borders. They can reach across oceans with the click of a mouse!

Innovative companies constantly encourage employees to think differently and to be creative. Forward-looking companies realize the key to their success and longevity is to harness this innovation energy. Innovation values the mindset that makes the impossible possible. I still believe in all my heart there is no better time to innovate than in the 21st century. The technological advances available to entrepreneurs today are unprecedented. For those of you willing to take controlled risk and be innovative the possibilities are endless. If you work today for a company and are employed, you at some point will be required to think and act in an innovative way. It's the one true competitive advantage.

You may be saying, "Yes, its great to be innovative, but what if I'm not creative"? That is a fair question. And to answer your question, I don't think innovation is something you either have or don't have. But rather a process you go through that looks at trends, changes and shifts in the status quo that drives the innovative force. It's a series of measured steps that takes current data against changes occurring on a consistent basis and then making a prediction of where this trend is heading. This provides the stimulus needed to move away from the status quo. The outcomes lead for many chances for discovery and once this cycle begins it becomes part of a consistent cycle of innovation and creativity. It's about creating a challenge to do things differently, exploring new territories, taking risks. There has to be a reason for rocking the boat. One reason for me that comes instantly to mind is the ability to download music or movies through the Internet. If you grew up in the 1960's and 1970's you knew the disappointment of buying a record album (yes, I did say record album for GenXer's) and only enjoying two songs out of twelve. The problem is that you had no control. You took what the artist and the record company gave you and had no choice in the matter. Successful small businesses and start-ups realize that change and innovation make a difference by enabling people to have more control over what they do. Hence, the surge in popularity in the iPod and TiVo technology that allows consumers to download, listen to, record and view the music and programming of their choice. They can have it anyway they want. It's putting the control in the hands of the consumer.

You need to think in these terms and begin to view yourself as an innovator if you want to create new products and services as an entrepreneur in the 21st century. If you plan to be in your own business, it's a prerequisite. Your clients will demand it of you! It will be important to set yourself apart. To offer consumers and customers new and innovative products, getting them to think and act differently. The status quo is no longer acceptable. We must innovate or risk becoming extinct.

Customer focus will drive this innovation. You must stay connected to trends in the marketplace. Consumers want more control and that is why these technological advances are finding such acceptance. All innovation should be focused on creating value for the consumer.

Interaction with customers and understanding of their needs is one of the best stimulators of new possibilities and the motivation for implementation. Remember, everything starts with an idea. The best way to innovate is to stay close to the customers that are going to use your product or service. It's imperative that you remove the blockers or stumbling blocks that prevent you from remaining innovative. The first one is fear. Fear does not have a place with a successful and innovative environment. If you or the people you employ are fearful of failing or of trying new things, innovation will die on the vine. People need to feel unencumbered by the fact that something might not work, but that is part of the process of innovation. It's about trying new things, exploring and if they don't work out, you learn from the experience and move on. Make innovation part of your review process when you evaluate yours or your employees' performance. Ask yourself and them how they plan to be creative or innovative in the coming year and then track their progress. Remember, you can't improve what you can't measure! You will also want to consider documenting the process:

- Idea Generation-This is the free-flow of ideas, brainstorming the possibilities. The ability to look at trends and gaps in the marketplace and then determining a way to fulfill these unmet needs. You want to gather as many opinions as possible and then cull the best ones. All ideas or suggestions should be accepted and respected. The group looks at all of them collectively and then votes on which one's go and which one's stay.

- Practical Application-This phase looks at all the practical ways this product or service can be used in the marketplace. The most fascinating aspect of this segment is the fact that you will hear ideas that you never thought possible for the item being discussed. Take the example of Arm & Hammer baking soda. The initial marketing was content for it to be a baking powder for cooking purposes. It then morphed its way into an air freshener for the refrigerator and then the company had you pouring it done your sink! Talk about marketing an item with multiple commercial purposes. You get my point.

- Manufacture and Distribution-How are you going to manufacture and distribute the item? How much will it cost to manufacture? What are your distribution channels? What is your marketing strategy? Can you market the item through the wed or is standard retail the best route? All valid questions that need to be answered.

- Marketing-perhaps one of the most significant events in the innovation process. You can have all the greatest innovation process and generate a plethora of ideas, but if you can't market the product, all is for naught! Thomas Alva Edison, one the greatest inventors and entrepreneurs of our time was probably the best example who understood that all of his patents (1,093) to be exact, wouldn't have meant anything unless he knew how to market and sell the commercial viability of his work. I emphasize the fact that you want to think about how to market and promote outside the traditional applications for your product and service. Think big about how you can market to the world!

- Modify/Enhance-Once you've established a solid customer base and have a good reputation, you will need to enhance and improve your product quality. You can literally start back to the first step in the innovation process. You will want to think of new and innovative ways to improve the product, think of additional applications, new market segments and additional distribution channels. You can literally create brand new markets for you product and service that weren't originally thought of during the initial idea phase.

Documenting the process will help you and your business create a consistent method of innovation. It will also give others in your organization confidence that you have a well-thought out process for capturing and utilizing ideas generated from the process. This process should be one of many that you cultivate for yourself or the people in your organization. People should feel free to collaborate not only internally, but also with others outside the organization to gain perspectives and to validate their ideas and suggestions. Encouraging this behavior gives people a wider view of what is going on around them. If you want a good idea, you need to be generating many different ideas.

It's important for me to talk about innovation in this book and in this chapter because I strongly believe that no matter if you read this book and decide not to start something on your own or you decide to start a small business, you will need to become intimately involved with the art of innovation. The world has changed and the demand for innovation has increased. You must learn the skills necessary to innovate to the point of establishing value through innovation. A good idea isn't enough. It has to create value! Creativity has been put into context as a tool of innovation. The end result-whether a new product, service, or process-is expected to deliver real value to customers and the bottom line. The two cannot exist separately.

Chapter VIII -Fostering Innovation and Creativity

The need to foster innovation with young people, I believe, will take on a huge significance over the next several decades. It will be important for parents to teach children how to create and innovate in this decade. And this is not designed to instruct them on becoming the next Edison or Michelangelo, however, if you do have one in your family, all the better! I'm talking about teaching them how to think differently, to think independently and to not be constrained by conventional thinking. The world they will inherit will be much different from the one they were born into. The demands on them in the workplace and even in their own business will be very different from the generation before them. They will be required to rely on their own ability to create their future and understand where their true talents lie and how to best utilize these abilities. The demands of the marketplace in the 21st century will require more from its workers and entrepreneurs. All the rules that have been in place for the last fifty years will be broken. The only real security that will exist will be in their own ability to know they can change things and make a difference. Entrepreneurs and people who can figure this out will be the one's who will be leaders in the future.

The "Art of Innovation" should be taught to children in school and at a young age. It should be part of a core curriculum along with math and science in the public schools. This is all part of an ownership society that President Bush talked about during his presidential campaign in the fall of 2004. The concept of ownership is about accountability and getting people to take responsibility for their future and their livelihood. The President talked about privatizing social security and giving people the opportunity to invest future social security benefits in the stock market. Allowing them to be creative in terms of how they want to invest their money. Innovative thinking is what will drive a lot of new inventions and entrepreneurial enterprises going forward in the 21st century.

I highly recommend building and teaching this trait in the home. Like any important life lessons that need to be taught, parents are the greatest teachers for their children. And just like teaching them right from wrong, how to drive, or how to balance a checkbook, teaching them how to be creative and to innovate will be critical for them during their lifetime. If you are willing to take this important step with your children, I recommend a process called Project-based learning. The process will help develop student's skills in such areas as problem-solving, critical thinking, visualizing, decision-making, cross-cultural understanding, and reasoning, as well as written and oral communication. Children engaged in project based learning will take responsibility for their own learning and in doing so will become life-long learners. And this is exactly the lessons, as parents, we want to teach. They will also develop better interpersonal and communication skills. Project based learning recognizes the varying abilities of the students, allowing them to draw form their individual strengths to work in areas of their own interest, thus giving them the opportunity to achieve at a higher level.

Innovation presents scenarios in which children are challenged to push disciplinary and design boundaries in order to create cutting-edge technology projects. Projects involving innovation can inspire students' curiosity and desire to participate actively in project design and building-so Innovation is ideally suited to be a starting point for project-based learning. This learning method is an instructional method in which students learn a range of skills and subject matter in the process of creating their own projects. Sometimes, these projects are solutions to a real-world problem. But what is most important in project-based learning is that students learn in the process of making something. They are totally involved in the process. They work in groups, collaborate and bring their own experiences, abilities, learning styles and perspectives to the project. In the course of developing a project, students decide on an approach by gathering and evaluating data from a variety of print, multimedia or Internet sources. They analyze and synthesize the information they have gathered and – in a cooperative effort – they determine the direction the project will take. Students then design and create their project – and learn to solve specific problems in the process. Technology can also play a major role in the project; students may use spreadsheets, electronic publishing, databases, email, and forum for research and communication. Throughout the process, the teacher acts as facilitator and advisor, guiding, rather than directing.

There are several steps involved for Project Based Learning:

Step 1: Identify a project idea.
Choose a project that will engage students. It's often useful to choose a project that solves a real-world problem for which there are multiple solutions. Try and make the project relevant to real life scenarios, so they feel they are making an impact in their present environment. Let the goal meet the standards.

Step 2: Define a plan
Establish a plan on how you will address the project and follow it through completion.
Make sure the plan is realistic and has specific goals and milestones.

Step 3: Determine the timeframe.
Establish a timeline that is flexible but structured. Set benchmarks for different stages of the project. Assist students in time management: Keep them to their schedule by guiding them through the project, and ask them to justify corrections to the schedule when they decide to change direction and follow new paths.

Step 4: Monitor the projects
Facilitate the students' process by providing resources and guidance. Help students define their roles and encourage them to assume responsibility while interacting in the group. Assist the students in understanding the project's parameters by asking them to identify their goals, tasks and outcomes. Remind students they are responsible for every step of the process and that this requires their total involvement. Assess the process as well to ensure standards and requirements are being met. Use rubrics to assess team dynamics and the project itself.

Step 5: Assess the outcome

Evaluate the project's progress and give students feedback on their understanding of the material and their teamwork. Allow for student self-assessment. Peer reviews can also play an effective role in the process. Also, encourage students to reflect on how the process itself has been valuable for them: This can help to design more efficient instruction.

Step 6: Review the Experience
Allow for individual reflection on a daily basis, perhaps by using tools like journals and idea books. Also, have group reflection and discussion. Discuss what has been learned and what needs improvement. Sharing ideas in this way can lead to new questions, and can also help students find new ways to tackle the project. Reflection can also give rise to new projects that engage the students even more successfully, since the new projects arise from the student's own experiences of problem-solving.

It's also important to share with children and students real-life examples of how young people have taken an idea and turned it into a reality in terms of a product or a service. When children see and hear real life stories, they become more believable to them. Sharing real success stories helps them to personalize and they can begin to imagine it for themselves. If they can't see it and touch, it doesn't seem attainable. So, when you are at the dinner table next time, share some of these stories with your kids and watch their eyes get wide with curiosity:

Innovative Story #1-Frank Epperson, a then eleven-year-old, invented the Popsicle and the invention was accidental. One day Frank mixed some soda water powder and water, which was a popular drink in those days. He left the mixture on the back porch overnight with the stirring stick still in it. The temperature dropped to a record low that night and the next day Frank had a stick of frozen soda water to show his friends at school. Eighteen years later-in 1923- Frank Epperson remembered his frozen soda water mixture and began a business producing Epsicles in seven fruit flavors. The name was later changed to the Popsicle. One estimate says three million Popsicle frozen treats are sold each year. There are more then thirty different flavors to choose from, but Popsicles Industries says the general flavor favorite through the years has remained "taste-tingling orange".

Innovative Story #2-For over a century, Americans have been enjoying ice cream on a cone. Whether it's a waffle cone, a sugar cone or a wafer cone, it's been and American tradition to enjoy a double scoop of your favorite ice cream. Italo Marchinoy, who emigrated from Italy in the late 1800's, and invented his ice cream cone in New York City, produced the first ice cream cone in 1896. He was granted a patent in December 1903 U.s. Patent No. 746971. Although Marchiony is credited with the invention of the cone, a similar creation was independently introduced at the 1904 St. Louis Worlds Fair. For folks who lived anywhere near St. Louis, Missouri, the biggest event in the summer of 1904 was the Louisiana Purchase Exposition, which took place in that city. No one knew beforehand, but that exposition was the occasion where ice cream cones where first made and sold. The person who did it was named Charles Menches and he was a seller of ice cream. But he didn't plan to invent the ice cream cone. Charles Menches sold his ice cream in dishes the way every other ice cream seller did. That August, when the Louisiana Purchase Exposition was at its height, was a real scorcher, however, and one-day disaster struck Mr. Menches. There were so many hot and thirsty fairgoers wanting ice cream that he ran out of dishes. And it wasn't even noon. He had more than half a day of business ahead of him and not a single dish to serve his ice cream on. What did Menches do? He looked around him and thought fast. Nearby was a stand where his friend , Ernest Hamwi, who was from Syria, was selling a Middle Eastern treat called Zalabia. Zalabia consists of a crisp, wafer-like pastry sold with ayrup. "Give me Zalabia!" cried Menches. He rolled up the Zalabia, scooped his ice cream on top, and presto! Ice cream cones were born.

Innovative Story#3

Spokes, spools, rods and reels…Playskoll's Tinkertoy Construction Sets, the tools of America's tinkerers were invented in 1914. Tinkertoy Construction Sets are one of the truly classic toys of all time. They have driven the imaginations of children for generations, proving that fun and stimulating toys never lose their appeal. The possibilities for construction are endless with Tinkertoy Construction sets. In 1992, to freshen up in preparation for the big 80th birthday event, Playskool unveiled a major redesign to this classic toy of motion and construction. The new, all plastic Tinkertoy sets featured brightly colored easy-to-assemble parts that allow kids to build bigger structures than ever before. Each set includes instructions to create vehicles that really roll, tall towers and even a free moving Ferris Wheels. Tinkertoy Construction Sets are the invention of Charles Pajeua, a stonemason from Evanston, Illinois who established The Toy Tinkers Company. Inspired by watching children play with pencils, sticks and empty spools of thread, Pajeaua developed several basic wooden parts which children could assemble in a variety of three dimensional ways. He designed his first set in his garage, and with high hopes, displayed the toy at the 1914 American Toy Fair. But nobody was interested. He tried his marketing skills again at Christmas time. He hired several midgets, dressed them in elf costumes, and had them play with "Tinker Toys" in a display window at a Chicago department store. This publicity stunt made all the difference in the world. A year later, over a million sets had been sold. Playskool acquired the Tinkertoy line from Child Guidance in 1985.

I hope these important were enjoyable and that you are able to share them with family around the dinner table. It's extremely important to share these inspiring stories with children. Magnificent stories such as these help to instill in children the possibilities of their imagination and what is possible achievable. Igniting a child's imagination is the cornerstone and foundation for them to do great things. Sharing stories as well as engaging them with games can help foster the notion of innovation.

The idea for innovation does not have to be centered on the notion of creating a brand new product or service. It can also be intended for someone to think differently or in non-traditional terms. The purpose is to get younger people to think about options beyond the path their parents took when they started out. The typical path of college, job and security is a paradigm that no longer has tremendous relevancy today. You have to think more independently on which talents you can leverage to create an income for yourself with out counting on a corporation or government to provide your livelihood and security long term. Being innovative in the 21st century is about getting young people to think in a different way about their future and utilizing their creativity to imagine the possibilities about what could be in their lives. And how do you do this successfully, you might ask?
Well, I'm glad you asked. There are many ways to instill this thought process in younger people. The most critical place to start is in the home. Children will have no better influence in the world than their

parents. It is absolutely essential that you, a parent, help significantly in this effort. But first, you must believe in it yourself. You must truly understand what I mean when I say the generation of children ages 12-18 will see profound changes in the way they earn a living. You must truly inspire in them the need to think differently about how they need to tap into their creative force and look beyond the traditional model. Share with them real-life stories as I did a little bit ago. Search the Internet, read the papers, look through magazine and trade magazine like e-week and information weekly. Search web sites for innovation articles and young people who have started small businesses and enterprises on their own. Share and talk about these accomplishments at the dinner table or during a camping trip or family vacation. Pick a time when you have their undivided attention.

You can also start an innovation club! It is similar to the cub scouts or girl scouts. You can model it the same way with monthly meetings with projects on innovation and visits to innovation centers such as IBM and IDEO, two companies that embody innovation. However, if those locations are not close by, there may be several businesses that are more local that would welcome a visit from would be innovators. The main point here is to give exposure to children to companies or small businesses that are embracing an innovative environment. Having children see and experience this would be a refreshing opportunity particularly at a young age. Hosting meeting at your house on a regular basis would help foster projects that encourage innovation and to get children thinking about innovation as a young age. Be careful not to start them when they are too young, or the message will get lost. I think someone at least 12 years old could appreciate the message and understand the full meaning. These changes and recommendations in this chapter are very radical in how we need to change the conditioned mindset. President Bush talks about the ownership society in which Americans "own" their future and have more control in what they do. I mentioned this earlier regarding allowing for young people to take apportion of their social security benefits and invest that money in areas of their choosing. It's interesting to hear the President speak in these terms of changing the attitudes of ordinary Americans, but I believe what they are proposing fits in line with the message of this book and that is to get people to take more ownership of their income earning potential and to not rely on the paradigms of the past. We must think and act differently in our approach. The "old ways" of looking at earning a living will not survive in the 21st century marketplace.

Another area to look into is your child's school system. Get familiar with your child's teachers, principal and school administrators. Understand the core curriculum. Find out what they are doing in the areas to foster innovation. First of all, it's always a good idea to understand your child's overall core curriculum. But it also might help to find out what they have planned in other areas for entrepreneurship and innovation. Many schools welcome outside help, like Junior Achievement. Programs such as JA supplement education by offering subject matter that is not normally taught in the public school systems. Finding out if there is interest through the PTA and parents might be a good way to see if there is interest in building a curriculum around entrepreneurship and innovation. It is better to go and survey the interest level instead of going it alone.

Remember, there is strength in numbers! Once you get a handle on the current curriculum and what interest level there is, there might be an opportunity for you to support an innovation program.

Innovation is getting a lot of attention in corporate America today and several schools are offering a core curriculum for innovation. From a recent article posted on Yahoo, The Institute of Design is one of seven schools of the Illinois Institute of Technology that has been teaching design thinking and strategy for years. It is currently supported by many of the largest corporations in the U.S. and it offers both masters and PhD programs in graduate design education. Corporate America has been sending its designers to the Institute of Design in Chicago to learn research methodology for a long time, but recently non-designers have begun showing greater interest in learning more about a field so closely associated with innovation. The Institute of Design recently introduced a nine-month Master of Design Methods (MDM) degree for management, engineering, and other professionals who want to be innovation leaders. The MDM will provide a background in design methods is user observation and research, prototyping of new services and products, creating systems of innovation, visualizing alternative futures, and linking user innovation to organizational strategy. The article goes to say, if this sounds very futuristic, that's because it is. Industrial design has evolved into a new filed—design innovation. Designing consumer experiences—information, interaction, and service—requires innovation.

The Institute of Design says it can help managers close what it sees as an "innovation gap" between the increased ability to create just about anything—thanks to the combination of sophisticated technology and overseas manufacturing—and the decreased understanding of quickly changing consumer cultures and ways of life. This is the heart of innovation—and very interesting stuff for managers.

A growing number of companies are installing chief creative officers, or COO's in their hierarchy, joining chief operations officers and chief information officers. Samsung has one. J. Mays, group vice president of design at Ford, has added the title "Chief Creative Officer ". Many companies are borrowing the title from the advertising industry to reinforce institutionally the importance of design innovation in their corporate organizations.

Executives can also educate themselves about design innovation by directing hiring design consultancies to customize programs for them. This quickly growing field is still a bit under the radar. IDEO, the Palo Alto, Calif. Design firm has customized innovation programs for Proctor and Gamble as well as Samsung and others. ZIBA design in Portland, Ore., offers the service as well, as do a handful of other design firms around the country.

If you are a manager at a company that's going to compete globally by playing the innovation game, you're going to have to learn how to innovate. Don't kid yourself about learning all you need to know about innovation in business school. You didn't. When people talked about innovation in the 90's, they really meant technology. When people talk about innovation in this decade, they really mean design.

Chapter IX-Don't Quit Your Day Job!

How many of us have sat around on a Saturday night with our buddies talking about how great it would be to quit your job and start a business. You know the one about starting a bar/restaurant in a Caribbean island and selling those fruity drinks with the little umbrellas in them! It's all about catering to a steady stream of tourists and vacationers who make you fabulously wealthy. Keep dreaming, right! I think many of us can relate to that story.

It sounds good after you've had a few beers after midnight, but in reality it would be a nightmare.

One of the classic mistakes everyone makes when they are considering going out and trying to pursue a passion! If you get anything out of this book, I'm telling you right now, DON'T DO IT! It's simply the wrong thing to do and statistics support it as well. You will be glad you kept your job and didn't risk everything. I know how many people feel; they can't stand their boss, the work isn't challenging, they don't make enough money and they get up every morning with a sour feeling in their stomach because they hate going to work. The latest statistic on American workers is that 47% of workers hate their jobs and hate going to work. Still, however, don't quit your day job! It's kind of an interesting piece of information and even more reason why you need to act upon the many recommendations in this book. You could be one of the 47%. It is a very disturbing statistic that many people don't like their jobs. It's one of the reasons I wrote the book to give people hope about alternatives and choices they can make regarding where they are headed in the pursuit of their dreams and passions.

But I digress! There are so many ways to start something on your own without quitting a perfectly good job. As a matter of fact I highly recommend it! Unless you are so independently wealthy that you don't need a steady stream of income, I would suggest strongly that you read on. You don't need the added stress of giving up your income and to jump feet first into the world of self-employment. I know it seems glamorous to just up and quit your job, tell your boss you quit and ride off into the sunset with your million-dollar idea and never look back. Well, let me tell you, it only happens in the movies. We need to deal with reality here. The key here is to not get overzealous and think that quitting your full time job is the only way to realize your dream of self-employment. Millions of people do it every day, pursuing small, independent opportunities without giving up a paycheck. It's actually a much safer way to do things when you think about. One of the key factors when a business doesn't work is lack of funds. If you have a steady stream of income coming in on a monthly basis, it eliminates the big risk of running out of money before you can get your small enterprise off the ground. Another important reason is that you will need at least two to three years of funds to keep you going while you engage in the new business. If you quit a job, there go the funds.

Remember, cash flow is a good thing. Also remember, if you have a significant other who shares responsibilities for bills, mortgage payments, etc. the thought of you leaving a job to start a brand new venture will seem daunting at best. Limit the stress to you and your partner by not quitting. You'll thank me for this later.

The key to make this work without quitting a perfectly good job is to find something you can do in your spare time (what's that!) and still have enough time to perform your regular job. Now don't get discouraged that it will feel like you are not really doing anything on your won. This can work and many people are doing it today. Starting off small and part time has many advantages; it allows you to learn and understand what it is you've gotten yourself into, understand if you really like it (this is important as many people start enterprises and come to find out shortly they didn't like it at all). It also allows you to learn from your mistakes without costing you a lot of money.

If you truly want to pursue this, you have to be organized and disciplined. It is not for everyone; however, if you are truly dedicated, you can make it work to your advantage.

First and foremost, you have to pick and find and idea for your part-time venture that will allow you the benefit of doing it in your spare hours, preferably from home. Selling books at your café and bookstore may not be a good idea since it requires you to be physically present. Taking the same idea and selling books and information over the Internet would work because it is something you could do in a part time fashion. For me, it was writing. I've always had a passion for writing and wanted to do something totally on my own. I wanted something that I could create from scratch and market it and sell it on my own terms. I've had this "itch" for decades, but didn't know how to "scratch" it. I spent many waking hours trying to figure out what was best for me in terms of starting something on my own. And most of you will have to go through the same process. Read books on starting a business, write down things you enjoyed as a youngster, talk to friends, bounce ideas, read the newspapers, articles and anything you can get your hands on that can help shape ideas of starting something on your own. The more ideas you generate, the more informed you will be on what's the right path for you. The most important key factor is to get involved with something you truly love to do! I know that sounds a bit cliché, but it's absolutely true. Did you ever notice people you meet in life that have a true zest for living?

They enjoy what they do so much that it doesn't seem like work to them? They are passionate about what they do and it shows in everything they do. People like that just have an innate ability to clearly understand what it is they were meant to do in this life and they do it with great ease. This is what you want to strive for! Find that one thing that you are passionate about, that doesn't seem like work and more like play and that will be the opportunity you should focus your energy and attention.

Once you've found the opportunity, don't underestimate the need for a plan. You've heard the expression: "Plan your work and work your plan". It's a tried and true statement that stands the test of time. My fear is that if you don't have a plan (in writing) it will be very hard to execute and to get you where you need to go. Put your plan together by starting with your overall goal. Make the goal lofty. For mine it might be, "I'd like to be a best-selling author and speaker with five books in publication by 2008! If you state a goal far out, it will give you something to strive for; a stretch goal so to speak. If you've ever caught the actor/comedian, Jim Carrey, talk about his early years as a struggling comedian, he wrote a check to himself for $10 million dollars for services rendered as a paid actor. He knew some day it would come true and that by putting it in writing it became part of him. Several years later he was paid $10 million dollars for his role in "The Mask". It's the power of positive thinking. It's a wonderful thing! So, start with your overarching goal and work through the details of your budgeting, timeframes, workspace, financing and marketing plan. You'll be amazed at how better you will feel if you have a written plan to guide you. And it's not to say that you cannot change it as you go along. As you begin go to follow the plan, you'll want to modify it as you get smarter at understanding and fine tuning your goals.

Plan on investing in a good home computer where you can load business-planning software. A good software program will help you with a head start on putting your plans together. There are many good plans out there to help you get started. These plans help guide you from the financial and marketing plans to a sales plan. As I mentioned earlier, without having a good solid plan, it will be much harder to execute your strategy.

So, let's recap what we have talked about. I'm going to give you five key points to remember:

1) Don't quit your day, no matter what anyone says! End of story. DON'T QUIT!
2) Decide on your opportunity
3) Make the plan and work the plan.
4) Execute the plan
5) Evaluate and modify if necessary

We talked at length at about item number one and I trust you got my message. Don't make me repeat myself! We discussed earlier ways to decide on an opportunity and I'd like to emphasize the need to tie that opportunity to something that is relevant and significant happening in the marketplace today. As an example, if you decide to raise chinchilla's and sell them in your area, there might be a very small niche market looking to buy chinchilla's in your area. It's not to say you can't make a business like that work, however, you will want to fully explore the marketing opportunity first, before you expend a large amount of money, time and effort. Narrowing your market will make it more difficult for you to cover your costs and to create demand. If you are able, try to come with an opportunity that has mass appeal and one that reaches a much broader audience. You will also want to try to leverage multiple levels of distribution. In other words, if you are selling chinchillas, the only way to really sell them is face to face through and ad in a local paper. Selling through the Internet or through television or radio may not be the best fit. Finding multiple ways to distribute your product or service allows you to reach more people more easily.

I know it sounds boring, but don't underestimate the need to create a plan and work your plan. It will help guide you through the entire process. Without a plan, you are like a boat on the pond without a paddle. Even if you don't like doing this mundane function, do it anyway or have someone help you do it. You'll be glad you did. The more information you can out down on paper and follow in a logical sequence, the easier it will become to execute your plan. For me, it was a matter of putting together an outline for the book and determining what were the major topics I wanted to write about, which eventually became the table of contents. Once I had the rough outline of the table of contents, I then focused on how I would construct my writing and put my thoughts together logically. Other areas I focused on were whether or not I would use traditional publishers or services offered by self-publishers. I didn't know much about either, so I knew I had to educate myself on the advantages and disadvantages of both. And I knew my research had to start while I was writing the book, not after. From my plan, I was simultaneously writing the book and doing my homework to determine what route was best for me from a publishing perspective. Another significant area for my plan was the marketing section. How do you market a book? What do I do to create demand? Who do I go to? Newspapers, magazines, and bookstores. My point is, unless I have a plan as to how I market the book, it won't get done. I need to clearly state my objectives and how I plan on achieving them over the course of my project plan.

Whatever opportunity you decide to pursue, you'll need a plan to move forward. Putting it in writing where you can see it and access it every day will be critical. When something is down in writing, you are more inclined to act and follow the task through to completion. If you have trouble putting together your plan and your tasks, ask someone to help you or start small so it doesn't seem overwhelming. A small, easy to understand plan is better than no plan at all. And don't get discouraged if the plan doesn't exactly follow what you have written down? It's ok to change and adjust as you see fit. Just because you initially put it a task and it sounded good at the time, doesn't mean you need to stay with something that isn't working. Change your plan accordingly if you don't feel you are going to meet that objective.

And I will end this segment with a subject we all love to talk about; finances! You will probably want to put together a budget of how much you are going to invest in your small business opportunity. Since you are probably going to start off small, you are going to need some start up funds. Where do you get the funds? How long will it last? If you under budget how do make sure you have access to additional funds. Is your spouse in agreement? One of the fundamental problems that many people face is they haven't discussed it with their spouse or significant other. Keep them informed of your plans and how you intend to fund your project. They will be much more likely to support you.
Once you've established your budget and you know how much you'll need, set up a simple spreadsheet to keep track of your expenses. I would include a fudge factor of 20%. In other words, if you estimate

$1,000, you probably need $1,200. It's frustrating when you under estimate and then have to go back and find more money. Better to give yourself some padding up front.

X) A Closer Look at Franchising

If you're like me, you'll go down this path between looking and franchising and starting something from scratch. For those of you unfamiliar with Franchising, think McDonald's, Wendy's, Jiffy Lube, UPS Store and Subway. Simply put, franchising allows you to buy into an existing business system with a proven business model. With franchising, all the marketing effort and business opportunity has been proven for you. The franchisee has proven the model works and there is a need in the market place for their particular product or service. In essence, much of the hard work of trying to define a market, where to place the storefront, what logo to use, and what equipment to buy and how to determine where your break-even is has been done for you. For those of you that are interested in buying an established system with many of the start up questions and concerns non-existent, then franchising might be the right choice for you. And if you've done any research on franchising, you know there are literally thousands of choices to pick from. It can seem like a daunting task. If you are serious about looking at franchise opportunities you should consider using a service called Frannet. I used them here in Atlanta when I was looking at potential opportunities. Frannet is a service that provides possible Franchise customers with a look at different Franchise businesses out there. The good thing about the service is they don't charge you anything. Frannet ultimately gets paid by the Franchiser, if you decide to purchase the franchise they recommend to you. The other good thing is they hold free conferences and presentation; usually on Saturday's to explain their services and what they do. I attended one here in Atlanta and it was very helpful. They walk you through each component of franchising and how it would affect you should you choose buy a franchise. It's very important to understand the "fine print" of what your initial costs will be, royalty payments and licensing fees. There are lengthy contracts that are typically set up between you and the franchiser that specifically outline roles and responsibilities for each party. It would be wise to read these contracts very carefully.

One service I really liked about Frannet was the personality and skills profile they conducted. It was extremely valuable! It involves a survey of your skills and interests and then evaluates the best type of franchise opportunity. The thing I like about it is that they didn't try to sell you on the "hottest" franchise or what was best for them at the moment. They were genuinely concerned about finding out what was best for you through a series of profile skills assessment worksheets. The purpose of the worksheets was to really find out who you are as a person and what type of personality you have. If you've ever been exposed to the Meyers-Briggs tests, these were very similar in nature.

The key factor you should be looking for is not so much what business is the hottest thing going at the moment, but rather which business makes the most sense for you as an individual. The key to your success in starting a franchise will rest solely on the fact if this is the type of business you truly enjoy doing. If it isn't, and you start it for the wrong reasons; hot opportunity, perceived returns, or your friend said it was a good idea, you'll be sorry you started it in the first place. Seriously consider a franchise only if it is something you truly want to do and because there is a passion from your soul. The folks at Frannet knew this was the right approach and after I filled out the skills profile, we began to look at specific businesses that were the right fit for me. It was determined that I was more of a sales and marketing type and businesses that were suited to me brought out my natural ability to work and deal with people on a regular basis. We then looked at opportunities that put in a storefront (think UPS Store) or something I could do from anywhere (web-based) that didn't tie me to a physical location and it was something I could do from anywhere. There are a number of franchises that fit this category, Home helpers (non-medical elderly care) as an example is something you can do completely from home. All you need is a good personal computer, printer and phone and your in business. Waterlessgrass.com was another such business I looked into that could be operated from the comfort of your own home. This business involved the selling and marketing and artificial grass surfaces to commercial and residential customers. Again, because of the nature of the business and its product and or service, there is no reason to incur the overhead of a storefront. You could do it right from your home. Another franchise business I looked into was an opportunity that helps established family business develops a succession planning strategy for their business. In essence, in a family run business, the franchise service helps them determine how they pass on the business and its leadership to the next generation of family members. Again, it's a business that can be operated from your home.

But then again, you may really want to open a storefront; UPS Store, Carvel Ice Cream, or a Signs Plus. You may like the fact that you have to be at a physical location and that your work place is separated from your home. You may want to see "traffic", customers coming in an out of your store with an added chance to speak with them and help them decide on a particular product or service that you offer. There is also pride in ownership in knowing you have a business or a store located on the corner of Main Street U.S.A. It's the American Dream, right!

Deciding on a Franchise opportunity or starting something from scratch differs from individual to individual. You will be the only person able to determine which selection is right for you. I would suggest strongly that you begin making a list of your SWOT- Strengths, Weaknesses, Opportunities and Threats. This will help you clearly understand where your skills lie and which one's you don't have that could be a detriment to your decision. Many people want the security of buying into a franchise system that has the "what ifs" and questions worked out. Remember, what we talked about earlier is that when you buy a franchise system, the franchisor has worked through many of the issues and hard questions that many first time business owners would have to figure out through trial and error. Many people who are just starting out in their own business like the fact these questions have been worked for them already and that they don't have to spend precious time and money learning the hard way.

On the other hand, there are many individuals who crave to be "the first" in their space. Who long to be an early adopter and create a business from the ground up? The completely revel in the fact of doing something that no one else has done before. They view it as a challenge and will stop at nothing until they reach a level of success. They also enjoy the challenges along the way. They don't mind learning by trial and error or learning from their mistakes. They don't view mistakes as failures, but rather opportunities to learn and grow and to do things better. They are greater risk takers and extract a certain level of thrill from entrepreneurship. They wouldn't do it any other way.

The key for you is to determine in which camp do you fall? Where is your risk tolerance?

How much risk are you willing to absorb? How creative are you? Are you comfortable starting something from the ground up? Can you sleep soundly at night with the level of risk? These are questions you will need to honestly ask yourself before you start down any particular path.

The Entrepreneur's Source is another great source for researching franchising opportunities. There are similar to Frannet in their approach as they help you look at your strength's and your skills as to where they might be best leveraged. One of the things I really liked about working with these services is they emphasize the key points about Franchising and they market those points well if you are seriously thinking about buying a franchise. One key benefit of franchising is brand identification with name recognition. Who hasn't heard of the UPS Store or Jiffy Lube or Cold Stone Creamery? These are the brands you see and hear everyday. There is a built in loyalty with these known products. A franchise owner doesn't have to convince customers of the viability of these name-brand products. It already exists. Customers naturally accept know products rather than one's they don't know much about. With a franchise, you are typically with these know products and can benefit from the marketing campaigns of not just you, but other franchisees as well as the franchisor. A new franchise owner can benefit from the proven success of others who are deploying the same business model. As franchise owners try and test new marketing techniques and new products all the new franchisees benefit together. You also benefit from discounts due to the fact the franchise has incredible buying power and can pass those savings onto you. And don't underestimate the advertising budget. If you go the franchise route, you will benefit from the large advertising campaigns the larger franchise organizations have in their budgets. When a UPS store spends millions of dollars per quarter advertising their store and their services, which do you think benefits? That's right, you do.

And the one of the most important aspects of a franchise opportunity is the support mechanism. Not only do you have the support of the franchise organization, but you also have support from all of your fellow franchise owners. The franchisor wants to see you succeed as it benefits everyone involved. Remember, the success of the franchisor is directly related to the success of each and every franchisee. You also derive benefit from sharing and working with other franchise owners on different ideas, best practices and new way to market your product and services. You literally have a built in network of fellow franchise owners who are more than willing to help each other as they are all after a common goal of success in their franchise location. It's a win/win! The benefits of this built in network are something you won't be able to put a price tag on. The exchange of information and help you will receive from others like yourself will be immeasurable.

Another important aspect of franchise ownership is the training you will receive. One of the biggest concerns of starting a business from the ground floor is the training component. If you do decide to start something on your own, your training will consist of on the job training. That's right, you'll learn by trial and error. The really isn't an owners manual if you decide to go on your own. However, if this is something that truly intrigues you and you enjoy this type of challenge then go for it! And if you go the franchise route, you can be rest assured that most franchisors offer training to help you in the start up and continuing operations. Typically, the training is delivered live or through a virtual (web-based) environment.

If you do decide to go the franchise route you might want to be aware of some interesting statistics taken from the IFA Education Study: Franchising currently boasts $1.53 trillion in entire economic output. This translates to 9.5% of the private sector in the U.S. economy. The number of establishments currently operated by franchised businesses in the U.S. is more the 760,000. Franchising created more jobs for more than 18 million Americans or one out of every seven jobs in the private sector. And, it provides for more than $506.6 billion in private sector payroll. Franchise businesses have a lower risk of failure and or loss of investments than if you were to start your own business from scratch.

XI) It's all about Marketing!

We all get up each morning from a bed and sheets that were marketed to us, brush our teeth with a marketed toothbrush and toothpaste, get dressed in clothes that were marketed to us, drive in a car that was marketed to us and pass dozens of billboards, and listen to radio ads along the way to our final destination. We literally get marketed to 24 X 7, 365 days a year every year of our lives. Early studies estimate children see an average of 18,230 hours worth of commercials per year before their 18th birthday. Corporations spend millions of dollars in marketing research trying to understand the best way to reach young teenagers with their marketing message. I just saw a recent article showing individuals who are leasing and or renting their "body parts", yes you heard me correctly, stomachs, foreheads, etc., for advertising space! It's a world gone mad! My point is that America is about marketing, and then some. Our whole entire economy is based on marketing. During the end of the stock market boom in 2000, consumers kept the economy afloat buy spending money. And why did they spend money, you guessed it, because they were marketed to. That's why. The U.S. consumer loves to spend money. It's why we have such a problem saving money. We do a great job of marketing in this country, but a lousy job of saving. Which makes sense? Since we do a great job of marketing, we tend to spend more on our families and ourselves. Unfortunately, this doesn't translate well to overall savings.

The Gross National Product (GNP) is the total dollar value of all final goods and services produced for consumption in society during a particular time period. Its rise or fall measures economic activity based on the labor and production output within a country. The figures used to assemble data include the manufacture of tangible goods such as cars, furniture, and bread, and the provision of services used in daily living such as education, health care, and auto repair. Intermediate services used in the production of the final product are not separated since they are reflected in the final price of the goods or service. The GNP does include allowances for depreciation and indirect business taxes such as those on sales and property. Total GNP in the U.S. is about $10 trillion, which accounts for 1/3 of the world's GNP. The U.S. has the highest GNP in the world and the second highest is Japan. We are nation of consumers and the GNP proves it out. We are the largest producer and consumer of goods and services in the world.

So, ok, Dan, you've bored me with all these statistics, what does this mean? Well, it's good news on two fronts, actually. First, because we are a nation of consumers, we like to see and hear about new products and services in the market. Americans are always curious about things that can make their lives better. Americans spend millions of dollars on products they feel can improve their health, their finances, or improve their self-image. We are a nation of people who are constantly looking for a "better way". We also pay large sums of money for convenience. People want more time in their lives. Time is at a premium these days and people constantly feel short changed.

They will pay money to have more time with family and live more of a quality lifestyle. If you are considering a business that caters or fits into a category that people are willing to spend, then you've essentially tapped into a need that people are willing to pay for. Once you find this niche and people show interest, you can continue generating a revenue stream for years to come. Because Americans love to spend, it puts a business owner at a good advantage. If you have a product at the right price and right place and satisfy a specific need, then you have the basic recipe for a successful business. The second benefit to Americans love affair with spending is they love to be marketed to. Yes, I know what you're thinking. I hate these ads and the bombardment of advertising. But the cold reality is that marketing works and Americans respond by buying. If marketing didn't work, Americans essentially wouldn't have a clue on how to choose different products, different pricing structures, and to look at competitive advantages among product categories.

Marketing essentially communicates the basic message of your product and service and why it's better than your competitors. If you want your business, product and or service to be successful, you have to market, you have to communicate, and you have to get the word out. People and consumers must know about your product, why it's good for them, and why they should buy it over and over and over again. I can't think of any better example than Coca-Cola. Coke has probably done one of the best marketing campaigns the world has ever known. Coke is probably the most recognized brand name in the world. And to think about it, it's not just about the drink, it's about a lifestyle. Drink a Coke with your friends, have a Coke to celebrate something good in life. Drink a Coke after a winning baseball game with your neighbors! It's all part of the experiences of life and weaving the soft drink into celebrating your successes in life. The marketing campaigns for Coke have been extremely successful at instilling in Americans that Coke should be a part of your everyday life. They've essentially branded Coke as part of American life, similar to Mom and apple pie!

There are many examples of these great marketing stories in America today. Marketing works on every level in the U.S. Take Intel Corporation. Intel was established in 1968 and eventually went public in 1971. During the 1980's the company developed the computer chips that set a standard in personal computing. In 1991 the "Intel Inside" branding program was conceived with the purpose of creating a consumer brand loyalty. By 1997, Intel controlled close to 90% of the world's market for personal PC microprocessors. Although the market is a lot more competitive today, Intel still maintains an edge as one of the biggest chip manufacturers in the world. During the early part of the 1990's, computer chips were pretty much unknown parts within PC's to most customers. Consumers basically don't care how a computer chip operates. They just want to turn it on and expect it to work. The company needed to find a way to differentiate itself in a perplexing and changing, goods marketplace. Intel discovered a way to do away with the vagueness of the computer chip while improving customer confidence that "Intel Inside" represented superior engineering and value. Using a clear branding strategy, Intel developed the "Intel Inside" program with a large group of OEM's (original equipment manufacturer partners. Intel also developed an aggressive ad campaign that targeted retail sales personnel as well as consumers about the importance of Intel's chip components without using "geek speak"

The end result to the end user has worked extremely well. So good, in fact, that potential buyer now consistently asks for Intel. Current market research show that 70% of home PC buyers and 85% of business buyers show a partiality for Intel and they will be a first-class rate for the protection and dependability offered by the product.

In 1991, before the start of the "Intel Inside" marketing push, the company's market capitalization was roughly $10 billion. By 2003 it had risen to $155 billion. In 1992, the first year of the "Intel Inside" program, worldwide sales increased to 63%. Among European PC buyers, knowledge of the Intel symbol grew from 24% in 1991 to 94% by 1995. And by 2001, Intel was listed as the sixth most valued product in the world, with a value estimate at $35 billion. Today the Intel inside Program is one of the world's largest co-operative marketing programs, supported by 1,000+ PC manufacturers who are licensed under the "Intel Inside" logos.

Nokia Corporation offers another interesting look at superior marketing campaigns among U.S. companies. Nokia was established in 1967. In the early 1990's, Nokia wanted to dedicate its efforts on telecommunications, its core business, by divesting all itself of all other operations. Since then, Nokia has put together a powerful technology brand. Nokia has become a world leader in mobile communications be concerning people to each other and the information that makes the most sense with ease of use technology products. As technology products and markets mature, the true exceptions between products become more difficult to separate. The mobile phone market is not an exception to this rule. The top providers, Motorola, Ericcson, and Nokia, were challenged to create a successful brand that didn't depend solely on features and functionality. Over the past few years, Nokia has devoted a concentrated endeavor to manage consumer perceptions of its overall corporate brand name. When Nokia positions it brand in the crowded mobile phone marketplace, its message always brings together the technology with the human side of its offer. Each advertisement and market communication conveys that message that "only Nokia human technology enables you to get more out of life". Even in the company's tag line, "Connecting People", was carefully designed to focus on the user benefit, not the technology.

The results have allowed Nokia to succeed in lending the personality of a trusted friend to its product line. The company has effectively displaced Motorola and is now the number one brand in many markets around the world. It now ranks #8 in the world's most valuable brands, making it the highest-ranking non-U.S. brand. And as of July 2004, Nokia's brand value was over $24 billion. Nokia now owns the "human" dimension of mobile communications, leaving its competitors curious about how to position them.

One of my favorite business turn-around stories is Harley-Davidson. Can you tell I have a connection to the motorcycle community in Atlanta! I've enjoyed motorcycles since I was a young boy. They continue to fascinate me, the sounds, the smells, and the feel of the motor rumbling beneath your body as you head down a beautiful country road with the smell of fresh cut grass wafting through your helmet. There is nothing like it!!!!!

Harley had been on the verge of bankruptcy twice sine the early 1960's. In the early years of the company it had a loyal following with leather clad clan outlaw bikers and a poor reputation for quality. Many Harley early owners remember spending more time fixing their bikes than riding them. By the early 1980's, Harley was bought by AMF, an athletic and sporting goods company. The purchase didn't do much to save the company's reputation and sales sagged dramatically during this period. At that point, several Harley-Davidson family members got together and bought the company back from AMF. Harley began its turn around story with improved quality and its overall marketing program to upper scale, professionals who had the disposable income and the fun memories of owning a motorcycle from their youth. Soon, Harley-Davidson loyalists began to come back and see the Harley brand as a lifestyle choice and started an organization called HOG- Harley Owners Group. It became cool to own a Harley and to support American manufacturing and ingenuity. During the 1980's and 1990's, Harley did a fantastic job of building brand loyalty and support among devotees to freedom and American values. The turnaround led the company to a healthy $761 million profit on revenues of over $4.6 billion in 2003. Harley-Davidson employees currently take a personal responsibility for maintaining the sparkle of the brand through activities such as attending rallies and guiding plant tours. Annual growth rates for revenue and earnings have been better than 17% and 29% each during the last 5 years. The company is ranked #41 on the 2004 list of the world's most valued brands.

You can see from the examples above how important and how critical marketing can be in your business venture. To, me, it's the difference between success and or failure. You have to remember that you can have the most creative, successful new product or service, but if people don't know about it, it won't really matter, will it? You have to tell people about. Talk to them and market to them at every opportunity. It's easier if you are the owner or inventor because you will have passion around your marketing efforts. Successful marketing will have a lot to do with your overall passion and belief in your business. People will sense that and will be more inclined to listen to you. Your enthusiasm will get them excited and will get them to buy your product. Come across bland and morose and you can essentially kiss any potential sales opportunities good-bye.

I'm sure many of you have heard about the "4 P's" of marketing, right? If not, that's ok. If your about to embark on this journey, you'll hear about it soon enough. The four P's of marketing include: Product, Price, Place and Promotion. <u>Product</u> essentially refers o tangible articles, services, concepts, beliefs and ideas. <u>Price</u> is the cost or other consideration that is exchanged in return for the product. It's a way of measuring the value the customer places on the product. Value must be communicated strongly so the price seems reasonable for the product. <u>Place</u> refers to a physical location, but can also be more than physical as it can refer to virtual sites, or simply how the product or service gets from origination point to the end consumer. <u>Promotion</u>

refers to all aspects of your marketing communication program, including advertising, selling and the strategies developed to get the customer to buy. Let's look at a recent real-life example and apply these four principles. EBay comes to mind as it a very good example of a company that embraces these four principles. EBay's product is a service. The eBay *product* is an on-line brokerage for buyers and sellers to come together in a free-trade environment to buy and sell goods at a fair market price. It completely embodies the American free-market system. Only it does it electronically. There is a *price* for those who want to sell items on the site and is based on the item, what type of ad display you use and length of time. For the buyer there is not a fee. This model is fairly typical for consumers who look to sell personal items. It's no different than putting an ad in a newspaper. The seller pays for the ad and the buyer of course is not charged a fee. So, in keeping with a good Pricing model based on the "4 P's" of marketing, eBay has satisfied these criteria in the marketplace and offers a "competitive price for their product. The *"place"* criterion is the really cool part. EBay is a virtual location, accessed by anyone in the world 24 days a week and 7 days a week, for 365 days a year. From a "place" standpoint, it doesn't get any better than that! Imagine having your business virtual where it's accessible to anyone, anytime, anywhere. If you have business that can be leveraged from the Internet, you will certainly come to enjoy the constant availability it affords. The promotion aspect of the "4 P's" for eBay was essentially done through word of mouth. EBay's model was not an instant success, but as people began to see the ease of use and the reach of people it allowed them to connect with, it really gained a lot of traction. Word of mouth advertising is sometimes the most affective and the least costly. The *promotion* of the item occurs through users that help to market the benefits of using eBay as an on-line tool to but and sell goods.

When you begin your marketing plan, it's helpful to keep in mind the "4 P's". They really are the guiding principles to any solid marketing plan. Pay particular attention regarding your product. Is it something consumers want and need? I know this sounds basic, but you'll be surprised at how many people forget this principle. Is your product recognizable and is it easy for consumers to understand the benefits and value? Are there competing products in the market? How do you plan to differentiate your product from your competitors? The 4P's are essential to your marketing efforts. If you are able to accurately assess the 4P's and how they will impact your business and the marketing plan, you've already got a head start.

Speaking of the Marketing Plan, let's spend a little bit of time talking about the importance of a well-thought out marketing initiative. You're probably sick of me talking about a plan for this and a plan for that, but trust me they do work. If they accomplish anything, at least they give you a bit of a roadmap to follow while you're trying to execute your overall tasks. You wouldn't plan a car trip or camping trip for example without a plan of how you were going to arrive at your destination and how you were going to return, right? It's the same thing when thinking about your plans for your business.

Your marketing plan should definitely include the 4P's of marketing, a project plan with timelines and assignments in terms of who will complete the tasks and how soon. Your plan should be realistic in terms of its overall approach and timeline. Overstating your marketing goals beyond what you can accomplish will only frustrate you in the long run. Establishing goals that are attainable will give you a sense of accomplishment once you've completed each one. One of the most critical themes to keep in mind when developing your marketing plan is how you cultivate loyal, repeat customers. Above all else, finding and retaining customers is your most important role in any small business. There is an old adage, it's easy to attract a new customer, but much harder to keep them. Your marketing plan should include a broad search for your customer base. Limiting customers to a certain segment or demographic could severely limit your sales potential. Think creatively when developing your market research as to who might be interested in your product or service. There may be markets that you didn't give consideration to before or overlooked that may have reason to buy your product or service. Think big and wide! You can never have too many customers, right?

Start your marketing plan with these components and you will be starting off on the right track: 1) Define your product or service 2) Define why customers would pay money to buy it. 3) Define a typical customer that you intend to market the product. 4) How is your product or service differentiated in the marketplace? 5) What marketing methods do you intend to use? 6) How do you measure which marketing efforts are most effective? 7) Act quickly in the event your planned marketing effort are not yielding results. 8) Spend some time test marketing your plan to see if it works before you expend a lot of time and energy. 9) After you've seen some results, compare your spend on marketing dollars to net sales results. The point here is that you could spend 3 X in marketing dollars and receiving 1 X in sales returns! That would not be a profitable way to spend your marketing dollars in the long run.

Let's explore each one of these nine areas a little closer. Defining your product or service is critical. If you can't do it effectively, it will be very hard for you to communicate its value and benefits to the marketplace. It's extremely important for you to completely understand your products benefits and value and why a customer would see value in purchasing the item. Have you satisfied one of the primary reasons why people buy? People typically buy to satisfy one of these needs: safety, health, financial, self-empowerment or self-improvement? These needs have been described in different ways over the years, but typically they always come back to those reasons mentioned above. Once you've determined which need your product or service satisfies, explore the value it will bring to someone and how the product totally satisfies the need above and beyond the competition. Also explore what attributes it contains that makes it a wiser choice among competing products in its category. If you can do this effectively, and be able to design an effective marketing campaign around the benefits, you have the makings a solid marketing plan. Once you do this, you will satisfy item #2 in defining why customers would pay money to buy it.

You'll also have to spend a bit of time on defining what a typical customer will look like. Are they a stay at home mother with kids that is looking for a better way to give their children more exercise? Perhaps your product is an in-home gym/playground designed for inside use. It's safe, inexpensive and helps children get more exercise because of its interactive capability and they get more use out of it because it can be used inside. Do you see how this example can help you define a typical customer and why they would buy your product? Differentiating your product can depend as much on the product attributes as it does on your marketing efforts. But be careful you don't over promise and under-deliver on the products capabilities. It's the quickest way to build negative equity among customers. It's a fine line in building the marketing "buzz" and the true capabilities of your product and service.

Look for the "unobvious" attributes of your product or service to define its differentiation. Most consumers will see the obvious ones. Look hard to see where your product satisfies a need where your competition doesn't. Once you find some key differentiators, you will need to develop a marketing plan that exploits these differences so they are painfully obvious to your marketing audience. A good solid combination of competitiveness differences and savvy marketing plan will effectively get your message across loud and clear. This topic also leads into a discussion of what methods you plan to use to market. There's a saying that goes, "Any publicity is good publicity". And perhaps the same can be said for marketing as well. But, this can come and backfire on you. Some marketing campaigns can go absolutely bust. Many a small business have gone bust trying to execute an expensive, ill-conceived marketing plan that costs way to too much money with minimal results. Please careful in your planning and determine what marketing approaches work best for your product. Buy some books at the local Barnes and Noble. I picked up several when I decided to write the book to better understand how and what would work best to market a book such as mine. I found out some interesting things.

I found out that just because you publish a book and it is available on a web site, people are going to automatically flock to the site to buy your book. No..No..No. It's up to me, the author, to effectively go out to potential buyers and market my book. I will need to do this through book signings, consulting engagements, developing my own web site and potentially teaching a course on the book topic at a local college. It's interesting how you may think one approach may work fine for your business or service, when in reality, what truly works is totally different. You'll find one of the best approaches is your personal signature. In other words, what works well for you and your product will depend on your personality. You may feel more comfortable marketing your product on person, in front of an audience or large crowd. Or you may prefer to write the copy and hire a spokesperson to do the speaking? Maybe you're more comfortable with a one on one interview with a local newspaper or radio program asking you questions about your product? It all depends on your personal preference and style.

Once you've found out which marketing methods work the best, you'll want to measure which efforts are working the best for you. It will be difficult at first as you try different methods; you won't off the bat, which one's are more effective than others. You'll have to try a few different approaches before you can begin to collect the marketing data. The best way to approach this is to make a spreadsheet outlining your marketing plan and the activities associated with each. Say for instance you've got three marketing approaches to your product or service. Perhaps the three you have involve print ad, radio and phone solicitation. You've determined these three methods are the best marketing approaches for your product and or service. For each marketing program you launch, you'll need to establish which marketing approach you used and compare them to each response.

Once you begin to do this, you'll be able to determine which marketing plans work best. If one approach is consistently working better over another, you can switch your efforts to the more effective plan. This will allow you to get a more effective response by focusing you marketing efforts that get the best results. Not to mention a better allocation of your marketing dollars, which in the beginning stages of your venture, can be very scarce.

It's important to look at the numbers of marketing. After all, it's about the bottom line. You'll want to track and measure the success rate of your marketing efforts and to react quickly if you don't feel you are getting enough return on your investment. Marketing, too many, is a misunderstood discipline. If done correctly, it can greatly increase your product awareness. Done poorly and you can expect limited results based on your dollars spent.

XII) Finding an outlet for your Creativity

Probably one of the most challenging areas for you will be to pick an opportunity that compliments your strengths and natural abilities. Studies have shown the majority of working Americans do not enjoy their jobs and going to work every day. Most workers live lives of quiet desperation. They go to work each day, tend to their mind-numbing tasks, collect their paychecks and hopefully one day, and retire with enough of a pension and 401K to get them through the rest of their retired years. In today's work world we all know it doesn't always work that way, does it? Most people, when they start out in their careers never really ask themselves that single most important question. Is this profession I'm about to enter something I'd want to do for the next 30-40 years? Not many people truly ask themselves that question. Most of us are too young and immature to really truly know and understand if this profession is something that will make us happy well into middle age.

As the baby boomer generation begins to move into their "retirement" years, they will begin to redefine what it means to find a true calling and meaningful work. Most of them would have been working since they were in their early 20's at jobs they may or may not have truly liked. And as they near the end of their full-time working career, they will want to be engaged in work that is meaningful and reflects who they are as an individual. They will want work to truly be something they enjoy and want to do. Most of them (if they planned correctly) will be able to pick and choose which direction they want to go. If they have saved enough money and did some good financial planning, they will have the luxury of starting a business and doing something they choose on their terms. The baby boomer generation will live a lot longer into their retirement than the generation before. With medical advances and better health care, many can expect to live 20-30 years longer once they officially retire. Their quality of life will be vastly improved from their parents' generation. They will not go quietly into their retirement. They will be active. They will want to learn new things and take on new challenges and adventures.

Many will want to start a business and realize a dream they may have been thinking their entire lives. And, now, at this point in their lives, they are ready. But, what do I do? What business do I contemplate? How do I know which business is right for me? What makes sense? What trends are occurring in the marketplace? How do I find a business opportunity that matches my skills and strengths? Well, if you're asking yourself these questions, you are certainly heading in the right direction. And to add in a shameless plug, the fact that you've purchased this book proves that you want and desire information regarding this important topic.

For me, it happened to be writing. I can trace a love and desire for writing back to my high school and college days. I remember sitting in my creative writing classes and hearing the professor give an assignment and getting excited about all the possible topics I could be writing about. As my mind raced with possibilities, I began to capture them in my note pad. I loved getting creative and choosing stories from my childhood and writing about my many memories growing up in an Italian-American household in the Northeast! After several rewrites and edits (all by hand before desktops) I would proudly hand in my work to the professor and anxiously await my grade. The anticipation would just about kill me. But when I got it back with a favorable grade and comments like: "WOW, great creativity" or Simply Wonderful", it would make my day. The pride of accomplishment I felt was beyond compare. I truly enjoyed this experience. Those feelings never really left me. Whenever I think about my college days and the pride I felt after receiving my grade back on a writing assignment, I am contented.

If you are about to embark on this journey to determine what it is you would like to do in terms of your own venture, don't sell yourself short. Look deep and do some soul searching for it is you'd like to do. Make lists of likes and dislikes. Go back to your childhood and remember what activities made you happy, passionate and excited! What were the things that kept you up late at night and made you lose track of time. Those are the truly enjoyable activities that can be turned into a business and that reflect who you are as a person. The best and simplest way to determine where to pursue your interests is to begin a list of your life. Yes, of your life. No, it doesn't need to be complicated. Just something you can refer to that lists out several hobbies and or interests that you enjoyed over the years. What did you feel good about in your life? What activities did you really enjoy? Did you feel a sense of accomplishment when you completed these activities? Did you look forward to doing those activities and did you lose tack of time when you were involved? Have your friends over the years complimented you on your skills and abilities regarding certain tasks, such as your ability to cook well or tend to the garden? These prompts and questions will help you answer some of the basic questions you might have about your abilities and where you should focus your attention.

Another way to uncover where some of your talents might be is to get involved with some of the activities or hobbies you are interested in pursuing. You've probably thought about these activities for some time and would like to get involved, but didn't know how. One of the best things to do is to get involved. Find a way to experience what it is you would like to do. For example, if you thought about developing a course and teaching, try and get a part time role at a local college teaching a night course. If you've considered starting a franchise, get a job in that franchise to get a sense of the business and what it is like to run an operation on a day-to-day basis. If you like writing, start writing down some specific areas of expertise you might have and determine how you might be able to transform that information into a book or novel. Remember, you've got to start somewhere and take action. Success only comes to those who take the first step! You can talk about something all day long, however, at some point you have to take action. You'll be amazed at how great it will feel once you take the first step toward understanding the route you want to take.

I'm a firm believer we all have certain talents and innate abilities. Most people spend their entire lives never fully realizing what gifts they possess and how they can share them with the rest of the world. The majority of people going to work every day hate what they do and dread going to work. Why is this, you may ask? It's simple. There isn't a match between what they do and their specific skill set. It's very simple. Most people don't understand they are not doing what they were meant to do. And to be quite honest, most don't know how to change or get to the point they need to be in their working lives. They will spend their entire working lives stuck in a rut. To be honest, it's quite sad. But, the good news is, you don't have to be one of those people. The mere fact you are reading this book is the first step toward better understanding what it is your good at and what type of business venture best compliments your talents.

Corporate America today spends a lot of time and effort insuring that its employees are in the right job. They want to make sure they maximize the productivity of workers. They know that people who are in the wrong job are not as productive and are not as happy as employees who are in the right job. Companies recognize this need, as should you! If you're going to do something and you plan to spend a considerable amount of time doing it, you might as well enjoy it! Right? These same principles hold true if you are starting something on your own. You've got to enjoy doing it if you want to be successful! Aristotle once said, "Where your talents and the world's needs cross, there lies your vocation".

Let's think for a moment of what actually needs to happen in order to make a reasonable attempt at starting something on your own. The first thing is to recognize you passions, what is it that motivates you and that you would enjoy doing as a small enterprise. Secondly, what external factors in the marketplace are driving a need for your product or service? In other words, can you identify a skill and or a talent you have that can be matched with consumer demand? Let's look at an example, shall we? eBay is a great example of how a business was built based on this criterion. EBay saw a growing need on the marketplace for people to conduct business over the Internet. The timing during the mid-1990 was perfect. Consumers began to embrace the Internet as a way to buy and sell goods electronically. It also coupled consumer's needs, who are collectors, to find a way to connect buyers and sellers in an easy, economical way. eBay provided that link. It also tapped into auction market mentality where people enjoy coming together in an "open market" where the market sets a fair price. With all these things coming together, it was a perfect recipe for success. If you want further proof of my theory, let's take a look at the explosive growth of the iPod, Apple Computer's device that let's you download music off the Internet. This product brings together several converging areas occurring in society today. The first are being customizable products to the consumer. The iPod completely fits this category to a tee. Consumers, over time, have steadily demanded products that are personalized to their tastes desires. Consumers today are smarter and savvier and they don't want products that are mass-produced. They want products that reflect their individuality and differences. Being able to download 1,000 songs that you choose for $.99 per song is giving the consumer exactly what they want in a personalized way. It also melds that love of technology and gadgets in our society. Consumers love to embrace the latest and greatest technology. With the Apple example you have another situation of matching a desired product with a desire in the marketplace.

But don't fret, you don't have to do the same thing as eBay or Apple, however, there are still many opportunities to create a matrix of skills and trend spotting that will enable you to do the same thing on a smaller scale. I'm doing something similar. I have combined a love of writing with writing a book which combines with a need to provide how-to information to a generation of baby boomers who during their retirement years will need and want information on the who, what, where, when, why and how on starting a small business. I have done a lot of homework and researched the topic well, so I am comfortable a need exists. I can't emphasize how important the research phase needs to be. If you think you have uncovered and identified a need, doing the correct amount of market research can confirm or deny your assumptions. The methods you conduct for doing the research don't have to be complicated. Keeping up with your reading of current events, trade journals, newspapers and the like can give you incredible insight into what's going on in the world and what might be the next big trends or waves in demand. It's this kind of information that will help you tremendously in finding needs to fill and then matrixing those with your personal skills and talents.

XIII) Conclusion

I trust in some small way this book and the information contained within has been of some help to you. I would encourage you to use it as a reference guide, mark it up, and make notes and suggestions in it as well. Use it as a daily guide as you plan your next step toward entrepreneurship.

I sincerely believe many employees today will become "accidental entrepreneurs". Employees and individuals who are making a choice about self-employment due to a desire to control their own destiny or because the availability of jobs is so scarce, that entrepreneurship has become their ultimate choice!

I wish you all the best success life has to offer!

I would like to dedicate this book to my sister, Marijane. She knew I was working on the "The Baby Boomers Guide to Small Business Success", but never got to see it in print.

She passed on May 14, 2010.

She will be missed.

Made in the USA
Lexington, KY
06 October 2012